The Suing Game

The Suing Game

Preventing and Surviving Class Action Discrimination Suits

Charles Carron

Writer's Showcase
San Jose New York Lincoln Shanghai

The Suing Game
Preventing and Surviving Class Action Discrimination Suits

Writer's Showcase
an imprint of iUniverse.com, Inc.

For information address:
iUniverse.com, Inc.
5220 S 16th, Ste. 200
Lincoln, NE 68512
www.iuniverse.com

ISBN: 0-595-17840-5

Printed in the United States of America

The Suing Game addresses the overall impact that class-action discrimination claims have on a business and suggests ways to reduce the risk of being sued. *The Suing Game* also suggests effective ways to deal with the media, customers, investors and employees in the event a class action suit is filed. However, this book is not a substitute for legal counsel and does not provide legal advice. Legal liability in an employment dispute turns upon the precise facts, the geographic jurisdiction in which the claim arises, whether the employer is a government entity or a private company, the size of the employer, and numerous other details. Moreover, laws and regulations change over time, as do the courts' interpretations of those laws and regulations. Accordingly, experienced employment counsel should be consulted to evaluate legal rights and obligations prior to resolving any employment dispute or threatened litigation.

The individuals, companies and other organizations mentioned in the hypothetical anecdotes in *The Suing Game* are fictional. Any resemblance to real persons, companies or organizations is entirely coincidental. Well-known interest groups are mentioned in these anecdotes for illustrative purposes only. Because the anecdotes are fictional, any actions or statements attributed to these interest groups are likewise fictional.

This book is dedicated to my parents, who taught me the difference between right and wrong and why it's important.

CONTENTS

INTRODUCTION

HOW ALLEGATIONS OF DISCRIMINATION CAN DEVASTATE EVEN A BILLION DOLLAR BUSINESS

A neutron bomb kills all the living things around, while sparing the buildings, the roads and the rest of the infrastructure. Small comfort since no one is left to use them. In America, accusations of discrimination against a business are like a neutron bomb. The assets on the balance sheet may remain intact, but the company's "goodwill"—and its viability—can be devastated.

This bomb comes in a variety of throw weights and delivery systems. Sometimes the company's attitudes toward minority customers are challenged as discriminatory. Sometimes, the issue is the company's treatment of its employees—or a single disgruntled employee. Sometimes unions exploit such disputes to help organize employees. Sometimes there really was discrimination; sometimes there was not. Sometimes the alleged discrimination leads to a lawsuit, and sometimes the company wins the court litigation. Usually, there is a pre-trial settlement:

Settlements in Discrimination Lawsuits		
• State Farm Insurance Company	1992	$250 million
• The Coca-Cola Company	2000	$192.5 million
• Texaco, Inc.	1996	$176.1 million
• Shoney's	1989	$132.5 million
• Lucky Stores, Inc.	1994	$107 million
• Home Depot USA, Inc.	1997	$87.5 million
• Publix Super Markets, Inc.	1997	$85.1 million
• Mitsubishi Motors	1998	$34 million
• Winn-Dixie Stores, Inc.	1999	$33 million
• CSX Transportation	1999	$25 million

Even government agencies are at risk:

• Voice of America/ USIA	2000	$508 million
• Federal Deposit Insurance Corporation	2000	$15.5 million

Curiously, it rarely matters whether the employer was right or wrong. The publicity surrounding the alleged discrimination often seriously and permanently disrupts relationships with customers, investors, and employees long before the real facts are known or proven.

Is there no defense against this weapon? There are many ineffective defenses. The most common reaction is for the company to deny a problem exists. The defect in this approach is that the absence of discrimination is not news worthy. You are unlikely ever to read a headline like this: "No Discrimination Occurred At Lakeside Motors."

The news media don't cover non-events. Even if they report a company's response to allegations of discrimination, the reader's interest—and memory—usually are limited to the claims of wrongdoing rather than to the rebuttal. Another ill-conceived response to a discrimination complaint is to blame others. Unfortunately, scapegoats have a tendency to exact revenge. Similarly, "confidential" settlements have a way of becoming public, at which point they are called "cover-ups" and do far more damage than the initial allegations of discrimination.

To illustrate the flaws in such typical defenses, this book offers case histories of three fictional companies, which have been the victims of the neutron bomb of alleged discrimination. These are composite examples, taken from a decade of headlines around the country. The common tragedy in all three cases is that the company's management—especially top management—misunderstood how this bomb works, and grossly underestimated its destructive power. Although some of the companies eventually found the right strategy, they lost more market share and spent much more on public relations and other remedial measures than if they had armed themselves in advance with the arsenal of effective defense weaponry.

Through these case histories, *The Suing Game* explores the right way to respond to accusations of discrimination, giving specific advice on how to evaluate a situation quickly and accurately; how to defuse media interest; and how to maintain the trust of customers, investors and employees. By following the advice in this book, your company can reinforce its core values of integrity, respect and fair dealing. In so doing, you can become the employer of choice in your community or industry—the employer that everyone wants to work for, and that no one deserts in times of trouble.

American businesses have crisis management plans for factory fires, product tampering, industrial espionage, computer system failures, and a variety of other risks, which occur with far lower frequency than allegations of discrimination. It's time for us to recognize both the likelihood and the magnitude of this risk, and arm ourselves to win.

I.   CASE HISTORIES

CHAPTER 1—THE SHIRT OFF HIS BACK

It started with a newspaper headline in the *Springfield Times*:

Tough Togs Store Strips Shirt Off Black Customer's Back

The front-page story told of Frank Ross, a 20-year old black man, who described himself as a regular customer of the Tough Togs store in Springfield. On April 18th, he was wearing one of their shirts while shopping for another. The (white) security guard demanded to see proof that he had purchased the shirt he was wearing, but Ross didn't have the receipt with him. Ross recognized the (white) sales clerk, who remembered that he had bought something the day before, but she wasn't sure it was the shirt in question. So the security guard made Ross take off the Tough Togs shirt, sending him home in his under-shirt. Ross returned to the store that evening with the receipt and reclaimed the shirt.

When Kyle Smith, owner of the Springfield Tough Togs franchise, read the *Times* story, he was outraged. He knew the real facts: The Tough Togs store in Springfield had a theft rate far in excess of the Tough Togs chain's average. Several groups of young men—mostly blacks—shopped the store almost daily, almost never buying any-thing. However, they frequently were attired in Tough Togs clothing.

At Smith's request, Tough Togs' loss prevention organization at the corporate headquarters in Omaha had conducted an audit and had concluded that only one line of merchandise in certain sizes had an unusually high theft rate, suggesting that a single person or group was responsible. In particular, the plaid flannel shirts in size Extra Large were disappearing at almost ten times the usual loss rate. The young black men who frequented the Springfield store wore that kind of Tough Togs shirt.

Smith had beefed up security, instructing Secure, Inc., the store's contract guard service, to challenge young customers who were seen wearing Extra Large plaid flannel shirts. In this particular case, Ross did eventually produce a receipt for a shirt—but there was no way to tell whether the receipt was for the shirt he actually was wearing on April 18th. In fact, shoplifters often buy one item, and then steal another with the same "SKU" number, showing the receipt from the purchased item if challenged. Smith was certain that's what happened in this case. Ross may have paid for a shirt on April 17th, but it wasn't necessarily the one he was wearing on April 18th. He may have been stealing the second shirt—maybe even planning to return it on another occasion, using the April 17th receipt to get cash back.

How did Smith respond to the *Springfield Times* piece? Here's what he said: Yes, the security guard made Frank Ross take off the shirt and return with his receipt. But when Ross brought in the receipt, the store gave Ross back the shirt. Smith denied any racial bias. In fact, Smith didn't see anything wrong with how the customer had been treated. Shoplifting is a big problem, increasing costs for honest customers. Retailers have to be vigilant. In short, Smith denied there was anything wrong with the way Frank Ross had been treated.

After Smith's explanation was reported in the *Springfield Times*, the local television news stations got interested and interviewed Ross, his family, his minister, his employer, and the local NAACP chapter president. All of the local media reported Ross' story, along with claims by other black customers that they had been mistreated at the Springfield Tough Togs store, as well as Tough Togs stores in other communities. White customers going in and out of Tough Togs stores were asked if they ever had been required to show receipts for clothes they were wearing, and they all answered "no." In fact, a white man in his early

20's was interviewed on camera leaving the Springfield Tough Togs store, wearing Tough Togs slacks and a plaid Tough Togs shirt. Extra Large. He said he often shopped at Tough Togs stores wearing Tough Togs clothes and no one ever had asked to see his receipts.

The news services picked up the story and several national television stations called the NAACP headquarters and Tough Togs' corporate headquarters for on-camera comments. Tough Togs' corporate media relations department in Omaha gave a very general statement about the high rate of shoplifting and the need to balance customer privacy with security. Tough Togs denied that any of its stores discriminated against minority customers. Nevertheless, the media coverage of the Ross incident grew and multiplied.

Sales at the Springfield store dropped precipitously, and Kyle Smith was getting angry telephone calls from customers, the shopping mall management, and civic groups. The local NAACP was quoted in the *Springfield Times* encouraging a customer boycott of Tough Togs. The local AFL-CIO affiliates joined the boycott, noting that some Tough Togs clothes were manufactured abroad, and none had the "union label." Tough Togs' corporate headquarters franchise division in Omaha was all over Smith to get him to "fix" the "Ross problem."

So Smith called Secure, Inc. and told them to send a different guard to the store. Secure, Inc. agreed. Smith also asked them to fire the guard who had been involved in the Ross incident, but Secure, Inc. wouldn't even discuss that topic.

Then Smith called the *Times* reporter who had written the first story and gave her another interview. In the interview, Smith acknowledged that Frank Ross had been badly treated. Smith said that the security guard had been out of line demanding proof that Ross owned the shirt he was wearing. Smith told the reporter that the guard was not an employee of the store—he worked for a guard service called Secure, Inc. that had failed to train its guards properly. Smith told the reporter that in his opinion, the guard was racially biased and should be fired. Smith invited Springfield's black community to resume doing business with Tough Togs. The *Times* reported all of this, and Smith figured the situation was under control. He faxed a copy to the Tough Togs franchise division. Everyone heaved a sigh of relief.

After Smith's comments were reported, the CEO of Secure, Inc. challenged Smith's version of the events. Secure, Inc. produced the letter Smith had sent them months earlier telling them to crack down on young black customers, who apparently were stealing merchandise. Secure, Inc. maintained that the guard had acted according to his instructions and therefore would not be fired or disciplined. Secure, Inc. said it was reevaluating its relationship with Tough Togs, and was considering a lawsuit against Smith and Tough Togs for defamation. Now the national media were interested again, and contacted the Omaha headquarters of Tough Togs for comment.

This time, Tough Togs' media relations department produced an Executive—the Vice President in charge of franchise operations, Glenda Fisher. Fisher explained Tough Togs' strong policy against discrimination. Fisher pointed out that the Springfield store was not company-owned; it was a franchise. Nothing like this had ever happened at any other Tough Togs store. The way Ross was treated was entirely wrong and inconsistent with Tough Togs' rules of conduct for its franchisees. Fisher would see to it personally that black customers in Springfield were treated fairly—or Smith's franchise would be terminated.

Smith was livid. He faxed the *Springfield Times* a copy of the loss prevention audit done by Tough Togs' risk management people in Omaha. See, it was corporate headquarters that was at fault here. Another call to the reporters and another round of articles and television reports followed.

Blaming others is news worthy.

A week after the initial story about Frank Ross ran in the *Springfield Times*, the national offices of the NAACP and AFL-CIO extended their boycott to Tough Togs' stores nationwide, and sales fell 25 percent. Tough Togs' stock, which was publicly traded, was down 20 percent. More and more black customers and employees came forward with new claims of discrimination, some of which were filed with the Equal Employment Opportunity Commission and other government agencies.

A potential merger with Camping Outfitters was threatened by the adverse publicity and diminished market value of Tough Togs. Tough Togs' principal lender responded to NAACP and AFL-CIO pressure by refusing to extend Tough Togs' line of credit. Other banks didn't want Tough Togs as a customer until the Ross case blew over. The Ross problem was the subject of a special meeting of the (all white) Tough Togs Board of Directors. They decided that the CEO would have to get personally involved and take the "high road."

Tough Togs CEO James McCauley retained the best public relations firm in the country and authorized a corporate image repair campaign—at a cost that eventually exceeded $5 million. On the advice of the PR firm, McCauley gave a statement to the media reinforcing the company's commitment to equal opportunity and announcing that he was traveling personally to Springfield to resolve the problems there. Once in Springfield, McCauley met with Frank Ross and his family, apologized for the way Ross had been treated, and gave Ross a $2,000 store credit to be exchanged for merchandise at any Tough Togs store. Newspaper photographers snapped shots of McCauley handing the gift certificate to Ross, just as Tough Togs' PR firm had orchestrated.

McCauley met with local community groups and the local and national NAACP officials. He assured them that an outside expert would be retained to review the security procedures at all Tough Togs stores—corporate-owned as well as franchise—and that no racial discrimination would be tolerated. McCauley also announced that Tough Togs would donate a truckload of current, first quality merchandise to Springfield's poor and homeless. The media attended these meetings and gave them wide coverage. A company admitting it discriminated is newsworthy. A company spending millions to make amends is front-page. Bums wearing yuppie coats made a great human-interest story, too. The PR campaign seemed to be working.

Everyone at Tough Togs heaved a sigh of relief.

But the NAACP, AFL-CIO, and various community groups did not desist. They complained that McCauley's actions were too little, too late—no more than "spin control." After all, why had Tough Togs brought in a heavy duty PR firm? Why had Omaha denied any responsibility for the discrimination against young black customers until the media ferreted out the loss-prevention audit? Why had Tough Togs denied that there had been prior discrimination complaints until the media uncovered the supposedly "confidential" settlements?

These stories got very wide coverage, because the media enjoy reporting about their own accomplishments. Tough Togs' sales and stock price continued to decline and the Camping Outfitters merger failed. Tough Togs' competitors picked up the slack in sales, gaining a significant share of the market—a much larger piece than they could have hoped to win through advertising or other marketing strategies. The NAACP demanded a "fair share" agreement from Tough Togs— effectively imposing quotas on hires and promotions of minorities and on minority ownership of franchises.

Frank Ross sued Tough Togs for $85 million. The lawsuit became a class action, which ultimately was settled for $40 million. Tough Togs' own attorneys' fees came to more than $2 million. Affiliates of AFL-CIO organized Tough Togs' manufacturing employees as well as the sales clerks in a number of Tough Togs stores.

Tough Togs CEO James McCauley was forced to resign. Tough Togs elected three minority individuals to its Board of Directors. Sales continued to erode and Tough Togs had a net loss for two years. The neutron bomb had achieved near-total destruction of a billion-dollar business.

What should Tough Togs have done to avoid this cataclysm? How can a company defend itself against the awesome power of discrimination claims?

TIPS FOR AVOIDING BIAS CLAIMS

- Have a policy prohibiting all forms of unlawful discrimination.

- Train all employees on the non-discrimination policy.

- Evaluate all employees on their compliance with the non-discrimination policy.

- Conduct routine audits to ensure adherence to the non-discrimination policy.

- Have a policy promoting "diversity."

- Have a routine procedure for investigating allegations of discrimination.

First, every company should have a policy prohibiting all forms of unlawful discrimination. For example, any retail company should have a policy that all customers will be treated fairly and consistently. Moreover, the policy should recognize that even the appearance of bias is harmful to business and must be avoided. It turns out that Tough Togs had such a policy, which was incorporated into every franchise agreement.

Like Tough Togs, lots of companies have such written policies, but they often are not followed. Why? Because managers and employees receive little or no training on how to avoid discrimination (or the appearance of discrimination), and they rarely are evaluated on this aspect of their performance. The Springfield Tough Togs store had no training program whatsoever for its sales staff. It was all on-the-job training, and non-discrimination never was mentioned. As for the security guards, Tough Togs' Springfield store had a written contract with Secure, Inc., but neither that contract nor the attached "store rules" said anything about non-discrimination.

Even if a business has the appropriate written policies and trains its employees on how to follow those policies, routine audits are required to ensure that employees are in fact complying. The Springfield Tough Togs store did a semiannual inventory of its merchandise, which required closing the store for a day and bringing in additional help to count and log every item—but the store never had done a single review of its employees' and contractors' knowledge of non-discrimination requirements.

Another problem with Tough Togs was the absence of a policy promoting "diversity." A significant and growing proportion of Tough Togs' customers were young minority men. However, all of Tough Togs' directors and executives were older whites, no franchises were owned by minorities, and there were very few minority managers of Tough Togs stores. The only minority at the Springfield store was the cleaner. Secure, Inc. had a diverse workforce, but both of the guards assigned to the Springfield Tough Togs store were white.

If the Springfield store had a diverse workforce, it's more likely that concerns would have been voiced about the biased theft-prevention program and it would never have been implemented. Perhaps a better system of electronic inventory-control tags, or surveillance cameras, would have been adopted instead.

In short, Tough Togs put itself at unnecessary risk by maintaining a workforce that was not reflective of its customer base.

Chapters 4 and 5 of this book discuss the essential elements of non-discrimination and diversity policies and how to bring such policies to life in a business environment.

In addition to promulgating and enforcing policies against discrimination and encouraging diversity, every business must have a game plan for responding to allegations of bias. In a large company, there might be a corporate compliance office to which every allegation of discrimination is referred for investigation and corrective action. In a smaller or decentralized business, the local manager—like the owner of the Springfield Tough Togs franchise—should be required to follow prescribed procedures. Even if discrimination disputes are investigated and resolved locally, it is essential for the headquarters to know about discrimination allegations in a timely fashion and to ensure that they are handled appropriately. After all, the value of the corporate name—the brand—is on the line.

An essential first step in dealing with allegations of discrimination is to find out what really happened. Let's say that Kyle Smith, owner of the Springfield franchise, had called Tough Togs' Vice President of franchise operations, Glenda Fisher, the day the Ross story first ran in the *Springfield Times*. Fisher could have undertaken an investigation of the incident, or at least instructed Smith on how to investigate it. Chapter 6 of this book describes appropriate techniques for such investigations. If there is an allegation that the discrimination is widespread or that someone high in the company is involved, the investigation will be more credible if it is conducted by an outsider—an independent attorney or consultant experienced in such matters. Because Smith relied upon Omaha's loss prevention recommendations, the investigation of the Ross incident probably should have been conducted (or at least reviewed) by an outsider.

TIPS FOR DAMAGE CONTROL

- Have a plan for responding to media inquiries.

- Accept responsibility.

- Acknowledge the seriousness of discrimination.

- Describe the company's zero tolerance policy.

- Promise a complete investigation and appropriate corrective action.

- Do not comment on facts, which have not been established.

- Conduct a complete investigation.

- Take appropriate corrective action.

- If the company was wrong, admit it and describe the corrective action in general terms.

- If the company was right, reaffirm the company's lack of tolerance for discrimination and describe how the company ensures compliance with its non-discrimination and diversity policies.

Meanwhile, what should Smith have told the media? That he was very troubled by Ross' allegations, and that he had already begun a thorough investigation of the claims. If an outside investigator was being used, Smith should have said so and explained that Tough Togs had given the investigator full authority to determine what happened. Smith should have explained the company's "zero tolerance" non-discrimination policy; if any employee is found to have discriminated against a customer, that employee will be disciplined, up to and including discharge. If a contractor was at fault, the contract will be terminated. If procedures are found to be defective, they will be changed. Chapter 7 is a step-by-step guide to media relations in discrimination cases.

Tough Togs' internal investigation would have disclosed that young black men had been singled out for scrutiny by the security guards. Regardless of the incidence of shoplifting, such a policy is socially impermissible (and probably illegal). In short, Tough Togs was wrong. Not necessarily about whether Ross was trying to steal a shirt on April 18th—but certainly in its approach to young black customers generally.

Armed with these facts, how should Tough Togs have dealt with the media? Fisher and Smith should have acknowledged that in responding to a particular loss problem in Springfield, the company and the franchise took the wrong approach by suggesting that young black customers should be watched more closely. They should have promised that all security guards—including contract guard services—would be instructed to treat all customers the same, regardless of race, gender, age, or other protected characteristics (and then they should have followed up).

Smith should have apologized to Ross personally and publicly, and privately offered him appropriate compensation for the embarrassment he was caused. (Although Ross might make an unreasonable demand, a settlement in four or five figures almost certainly was possible at this early stage.) Smith should have encouraged any other Springfield residents concerned about their treatment at the Tough Togs store to call him personally. Chapter 8 is a guide to remedying real and perceived discrimination while building trust with customers, employees and other stakeholders.

After the media reported Fisher's and Smith's apologies and their promises to correct the situation, there probably would have been no further media interest in the Ross case. The public usually accepts a mistake, which is acknowledged and corrected because there has been no breach of trust—whereas the public does not forgive a business that initially denies the existence of a problem or blames others for it.

Let's say that Tough Togs revitalizes its non-discrimination and diversity policies and a year later, another young black customer, Tom Landers, complains of race discrimination, hoping to jump on the Ross bandwagon. After a thorough investigation, Tough Togs concludes that there was absolutely no discrimination. Unlike Ross, Landers was observed via a closed circuit television taking the inventory control tag off a shirt in the store and putting it in a shopping bag with other merchandise he already had purchased. He was apprehended as he walked out of the store without paying for the shirt. How should Tough Togs respond to Landers' allegations of race discrimination?

In this case, Tough Togs should be emphatic that its non-discriminatory policies were followed, and that there was no discrimination against Landers. At the same time, Fisher and Smith should acknowledge that when an incident like this occurs, it often seems to the community that one group is being singled out, even when that is not happening. Fisher and Smith should describe Tough Togs' non-discrimination and diversity policies, how the policies are disseminated, how employees are trained, how audits are conducted to determine whether the policy is being followed, and so forth. If there has been a recent audit—perhaps using "mystery shoppers" of different races to make sure customers are being treated fairly—Fisher and Smith could share the results of that audit. If Tough Togs has conducted race-sensitive customer satisfaction surveys, which have comparable results for black and white customers, the survey results could be shared publicly.

The media are likely to lose interest in the Landers case if Tough Togs validates the importance of the allegations of discrimination and accepts responsibility for avoiding discrimination—which is far different from simply denying that anything wrong ever happens or blaming others when it does.

The lesson of this case history—and the rest of this book—is that you can't keep people from bombing your company with allegations of discrimination, but you can neutralize that "neutron bomb" if you know how.

CHAPTER 2—NO SHIRT, NO SERVICE

Hispanics Claim MochaJava Wouldn't Serve Them

The MochaJava coffee house was the one place you could go in the beach town of Waterside and find all kinds of people. The owners, Phyllis Maize and Sara Corning, were an openly lesbian couple. They hired a diverse staff, and the manager was Asian—Margaret Chan.

The clientele was equally diverse. Teenagers, retirees, white people, people of color, straight and gay, all came to MochaJava for coffee and light meals. Maize and Corning kept MochaJava's prices low—undercutting the national chains like Starbucks—and that kept the restaurant almost full day and night. Turnover of the wait staff was a problem because the modest customer bills didn't generate high tips. But Waterside was a beach town with a steady supply of new, inexperienced employees who would work for the restaurant sub-minimum wage and the meager tips until they found better jobs and moved on.

It was Saturday night of the July 4th weekend and the phone was ringing when Maize and Corning got home from a party. It was Bart Hopkins, the attorney who had done legal work for the women when they opened the restaurant. Hopkins was calling with a "head's up." He had just declined to represent Arturo San Francisco and four of his friends, all Hispanic, who wanted to sue MochaJava for denying them service due to their national origin. Hopkins had turned down the case because of the potential conflict of interest. Hopkins figured they would get another attorney, in Waterside or the next town, to represent them and thought the owners would

15

want to be prepared. Unfortunately, he had heard too much of San Francisco's version of the facts to represent MochaJava. It was an awkward situation.

Corning called the restaurant. The doors were closed, but the kitchen staff were still cleaning up and Chan was preparing the night deposit for the bank. Corning and Maize asked Chan to stay and they drove down to the restaurant to talk to her.

Chan figured what it was about. She had planned to call the owners Sunday morning to tell them about her confrontation with the Hispanic man and his friends. Sitting in a booth, Chan told Corning and Maize what had happened. Chan spoke very softly, and occasionally Corning or Maize had to ask her to speak up.

Chan related the incident. She was relieving the cashier at the front of the restaurant when a Hispanic man barged in front of the customers in line to pay their checks and got right in Chan's face. He was using profanity and complaining vaguely about being "dissed." All the customers in the restaurant were listening to him. Chan figured he probably was drunk or on some drugs, he was so abusive. Chan didn't know what the man's problem was, but she did know that if she didn't get him out of the restaurant, other customers were going to leave, and MochaJava would lose a big day of business.

Before Chan could say anything to the man (who turned out to be San Francisco), two other Hispanic men and two Hispanic women had pushed to the front of the cashier's line and were standing right next to the abusive man. They were leaning over the cash register counter, practically touching Chan. She was afraid. She wanted them to leave, but she felt intimidated.

One of the men had a large tattoo on his chest. No shirt. Chan told that man he would have to put on a shirt or leave the restaurant. He swore something in Spanish. Chan reiterated that the restaurant required customers to wear shirts, and unless he put one on, he would have to leave. San Francisco started to argue with Chan, but the man without the shirt stormed out of the restaurant. San Francisco and the other three followed him to the street. Through the plate glass window, Chan could see that they were still in front of the restaurant, gesturing angrily and occasionally staring into the restaurant. Then they walked the length of the plate glass windows, staring at customers sitting at the front tables. One of the Hispanic women was taking notes on a small notepad.

Chan, afraid of violence, called the police. The Hispanic customers walked away before the police arrived. Two officers came into the restaurant, and Chan gave them a statement. Chan showed the officers the sign posted on the restaurant door:

> # No shirt, no shoes, no service
> # No sleeveless shirts for men

Chan reminded Maize and Corning that when Chan first became manager of the restaurant, it was common for MochaJava to serve men without shirts. But Maize had told Chan that there had been complaints from some regular customers about shirt-less men, and Maize had asked Chan and the wait staff to enforce the rule.

According to Chan, the Hispanic man was the only one without a shirt in the restaurant in a long time.

Maize had been taking notes while Chan was telling her story. She asked Chan to read the notes and to correct anything that was inaccurate. Chan made a few minor changes. She took out the part about telling the man he could put on a shirt. Maize asked Chan to sign the notes, but Chan declined, saying she didn't know if she was supposed to do that. Corning and Maize thanked Chan for what must have been a horrible day for her. They offered to drive Chan to the bank for the night deposit and then drive her home, and Chan accepted. They didn't talk in the car.

The summer season ended and nothing came of the incident. Chan and most of the wait staff moved out of the area.

After Labor Day, the sheriff served a Summons and Complaint on Maize, and another on Corning, in a lawsuit that had been filed by San Francisco on behalf of himself and his friends. The Complaint included the following allegations:

- Plaintiffs placed their orders for food and beverages at approximately 1:30 p.m.
- Neither food nor beverages were served to plaintiffs between 1:30 p.m. and 1:45 p.m.
- At approximately 1:45 p.m., plaintiff San Francisco asked the waiter (name unknown) when their drinks would be served.
- The waiter responded that their drinks would be served when they [i.e., the drinks] were ready.
- Non-Hispanic customers who had placed orders after 1:30 p.m. were served their drinks prior to 1:45 p.m.
- Neither food nor beverages were served to plaintiffs between 1:45 p.m. and 1:55 p.m.
- At approximately 1:55 p.m., plaintiff San Francisco again asked the waiter when their drinks would be served, and when their food would be served.
- The waiter responded that their drinks and food would be served when they [i.e., the food and the drinks] were ready.
- Non-Hispanic customers who had placed orders after 1:30 p.m. were served their food prior to 1:55 p.m.
- Neither food nor beverages were served to plaintiffs between 1:55 p.m. and 2:05 p.m.
- At approximately 2:05 p.m., plaintiff San Francisco again asked the waiter when plaintiffs' drinks and food would be served.
- The waiter responded, "Don't you understand English? I told you I'll serve you when your orders are up. I don't run the kitchen." or words to that effect.

- Neither food nor beverages were served to plaintiffs between 2:05 p.m. and 2:15 p.m.
- At approximately 2:15 p.m., plaintiff San Francisco asked the waiter who the manager of the restaurant was.
- The waiter pointed at the woman standing at the cash register, whom plaintiffs subsequently learned was defendant Margaret Chan.
- At approximately 2:15 p.m., plaintiff San Francisco asked defendant Chan if he could speak with her privately about a problem.
- Defendant Chan ignored plaintiff San Francisco and continued to ring up the checks of other customers.
- Plaintiff San Francisco began to describe to defendant Chan the problem plaintiffs had experienced but defendant Chan told plaintiff San Francisco she could not talk to him now because she was ringing up the other customers.
- The remaining plaintiffs joined plaintiff San Francisco at the cash register.
- Defendant Chan abruptly and loudly told plaintiff Gonzalez that he would have to leave the restaurant because he was not wearing a shirt.
- Plaintiff Gonzalez offered to put on a shirt that he had in his backpack.
- Defendant Chan told plaintiff Gonzalez "it's too late, you already broke the rule and you have to leave," or words to that effect.
- Plaintiff Gonzalez began to get his shirt out of his backpack.
- Defendant Chan told plaintiff Gonzalez "you've got to leave now or I'm calling the police," or words to that effect.
- On information and belief, many other customers present at the MochaJava restaurant at the time heard what Defendant Chan said to plaintiff Gonzalez.
- Plaintiffs left the restaurant.

- After leaving the restaurant, plaintiffs looked through the restaurant windows and observed numerous non-Hispanic customers wearing sleeveless shirts, and in all cases, food and beverages had been served to them and others at their tables.
- In particular, at the window table third to the left of the restaurant's front door, a non-Hispanic man who was wearing a string-type tank top shirt, had been served food and beverage. His shirt did not cover his arms, his shoulders (other than the two "strings"), or his chest between his neck and the middle of his pectoral muscles.
- On information and belief, on numerous other occasions, non-Hispanic men without shirts have been served food and beverages at the MochaJava restaurant, and have not been told to leave.

Chan had moved out of state, and had not provided a forwarding address. Corning and Maize interviewed the wait staff who had been working July 4th weekend, but none of them remembered the incident at all.

Armed with the written notes of their interview with Chan, Corning and Maize answered the Complaint by denying any discrimination and many of the factual allegations. They didn't look forward to the trial. Their (new) lawyer, Francine Jacobs, told them that their notes of the interview with Chan weren't admissible into evidence, so they would have to pay a "skip tracer" to find her—and the waiter if they could figure out who that was. Jacobs probably would have to travel to wherever Chan and the waiter were now living to take their depositions, which would be expensive. Didn't Corning and Maize want to settle? They authorized Jacobs to initiate settlement discussions with the plaintiffs' lawyer, Joel Tillman, who was with a big-city firm hundreds of miles away.

Tillman had taken the case for free ("pro bono"). He typically defended discrimination cases on behalf of large corporations. This case seemed like a good opportunity to balance the scales of justice.

Besides, the trial—if the case went to trial—was likely to be in the summer and Tillman was looking forward to spending some time in Waterside when the surf was up.

Jacobs' inquiry about settlement was music to Tillman's ears. He figured the MochaJava restaurant must have a guilty conscience. Pity it was a one-of-a-kind restaurant rather than a chain; Tillman would have liked the excitement and publicity of a class action.

Jacobs wanted Tillman's clients to make a settlement offer. Tillman was ready for this, and said his clients wanted a million dollars—not out of line for settlements in similar cases where the plaintiffs had been publicly humiliated. Jacobs told Tillman he thought the offer was absurd, but he would convey it to his clients.

Corning and Maize rejected the offer, of course. Even if they had a bad case, it wasn't worth that kind of money (was it?). Besides, they didn't have that kind of money and they weren't insured for discrimination claims. Jacobs asked if they wanted to counteroffer. They decided not to make a counteroffer because that would just invite the plaintiffs to "split the difference," and half a million dollars was still impossible. Corning and Maize asked Jacobs how she thought the case would come out if there were a trial. Jacobs thought they could get a jury verdict against them in six figures. Corning and Maize were sick at the prospect of losing their life savings—and maybe their house—over this nuisance suit.

When Tillman told San Francisco and his co-plaintiffs that MochaJava wasn't even making a counteroffer, they felt disrespected. Tillman explained to them, as he had several times already, that even if they won a large verdict against MochaJava, they could expect difficulty collecting their judgment. Although MochaJava was a partnership rather than a corporation, which meant they could go against the owners' assets, it wasn't apparent that Corning and Maize had lots of money. Perhaps they should ask for a modest settlement, with an apology.

San Francisco accused Tillman of being insensitive to Hispanics, of selling them out. Tillman got angry at San Francisco for being ungrateful. Eventually they apologized to each other. San Francisco told Tillman that MochaJava was just a symptom of the systemic discrimination against Hispanic consumers in Waterside, especially in restaurants, hotels and clubs. San Francisco and his co-plaintiffs had been mistreated at a number of Waterside's eateries and they had friends from out of state who had been discriminated against at a couple of Waterside's hotels when they had come to visit.

Tillman talked to a couple of his law partners and they agreed that expanding the case to include other "public accommodations" in Waterside would give the case more impact. Other restaurants, as well as clubs and hotels, could be brought in as defendants. But they would need additional plaintiffs too—individuals who had been discriminated against by each of the new defendants. How would they find the plaintiffs? Lawyers could advertise their services, but soliciting clients was still a violation of the ethical rules of the state Bar Association.

San Francisco and his co-plaintiffs started hand-billing MochaJava and a variety of other "public accommodations" in Waterside. Their handbills described their lawsuit against MochaJava and gave Jacobs' name and phone number for individuals who "wanted more information." The local newspaper and television station covered the hand-billing. Although the flyers did not invite additional plaintiffs to join their lawsuit, the calls started coming in.

The media reports were very even-handed. They covered the Hispanic customers' allegations and Corning and Maize's denials. Still, business at MochaJava fell precipitously, even compared to the previous year's off-season figures.

Eight more Hispanic consumers joined San Francisco's lawsuit as named plaintiffs, and they added twenty Waterside businesses as defendants. The thirteen named plaintiffs sought to represent a class of all Hispanic customers of the twenty-one Waterside businesses. Some of those businesses were franchises of national companies, and Tillman was working on bringing those companies in as defendants.

Media coverage was frequent and intense, and now national. Prospective plaintiffs were calling from all around the country.

Corning and Maize were able to trace Chan, but she was thousands of miles away and would not cooperate with them. To subpoena her to give a deposition would require retaining a lawyer in her state and filing an ancillary lawsuit. Jacobs advised against this because she didn't expect Chan's testimony to be helpful because of her hostility. Corning and Maize never did figure out which waiter had served San Francisco and his friends.

Media coverage continued and the Hispanic Association on Corporate Responsibility called for a boycott of MochaJava and the other Waterside businesses that had been sued. NAACP joined the boycott and recommended that convention groups go to communities other than Waterside. Business at Waterside's "public accommodations," even among white Anglo customers, fell almost 30 percent, despite 2-for-1 specials and other promotions designed to lure back customers.

Eventually, the Waterside businesses that were defendants in the lawsuit contributed according to their revenues and raised the $5 million necessary to settle the lawsuit. San Francisco and the other named plaintiffs each got $100,000, and the rest was paid in $100 increments to each minority customer who claimed to have received discriminatory service at a Waterside public accommodation during the past two years.

In the settlement, MochaJava and the other defendants also agreed to goals and timetables for increasing numbers of Hispanic and black restaurant managers. The national companies set aside $10 million to sponsor minority-owned franchises.

How could this result have been avoided?

First, MochaJava's owners, Corning and Maize, should have done a better job of publicizing a non-discrimination policy and ensuring that all their employees knew and followed the policy. This is as important for a small business as for a large company—perhaps more important because the owners' personal assets may be on the line.

Second, once San Francisco complained to Chan, she should have taken the situation much more seriously. She should have realized that a dissatisfied customer—even an irate customer—needs to have his or her concerns recognized and validated. She should have asked another employee to cover the cash register while she talked to San Francisco privately. Or if no one else was available to cover the register, she should have told San Francisco that she wanted to talk to him and could meet with him as soon as the cashier returned from her break. A demonstration of respect could have defused the entire situation.

After listening to San Francisco, Chan might have been able to satisfy him by apologizing for the lousy service and offering him some compensation—perhaps a free meal on another occasion for him and his group. Regardless of how the encounter with San Francisco went, Chan also should have notified the owners of the restaurant immediately.

Third, MochaJava should have had a game plan for responding to allegations of discrimination. Chapters 6 through 8 have detailed guidance on these topics. At the very least, the allegations of discrimination needed to be investigated. Because Chan was accused, she could not be the investigator. Corning or Maize, or better yet their attorney, should have interviewed Chan and the waiter. A trained investigator, or an attorney, would have seen the significance of Chan recanting the part of her story that had to do with asking Gonzalez to put on a shirt. There's a big difference between telling a customer, "If you want to stay you have to put on a shirt" versus "You have to leave because you weren't wearing a shirt."

Even if the investigation failed to establish that any discriminatory conduct occurred, Chan and the waiter should have been required, as a condition of continued employment, to sign notarized affidavits about what happened and to acknowledge their understanding of MochaJava's non-discrimination policy.

Fourth, when confronted by the media, Chan or the owners of the restaurant should have stated that they did not tolerate any discrimination in the restaurant, that they were taking the allegations very seriously, and that a detailed investigation would be (or had been) conducted.

Let's say that after a thorough, impartial investigation, it was determined that San Francisco and his friends were not discriminated against on the basis of race or national origin. The waiter was not motivated by the fact that the customers were Hispanic. Rather, the restaurant was understaffed that day and the waiter was in a bad mood. He had forgotten to put in their order. Then, San Francisco was so loud and demanding, that the waiter decided to hold off a few more minutes putting in their order. Anyway, San Francisco and his friends were only ordering coffee and rolls, which meant a small tip. It had nothing to do with their being Hispanic. The waiter just didn't like them and the way they were treating him. He didn't give good service to customers who "dissed" him.

Even if this was what actually occurred, San Francisco and his friends got bad service (or no service) and Chan should have apologized for that. Clearly, Chan should not have required the group to leave because Gonzalez was shirt-less, given the bad service they had received and the spotty enforcement of the dress code in the past.

But even if Chan had made Gonzalez leave because he hadn't been wearing a shirt, Maize and Corning could have salvaged the situation once they were sued. Because the no-shirt/no-service rule had not been consistently enforced, and at least one other customer who violated the dress code had in fact received service that day, MochaJava was wrong in this case. Corning and Maize should have admitted fault, even if the customers were not discriminated against because of being Hispanic. Regardless of whether bias occurred in this case, they should have apologized for the bad service—even before trying to settle the lawsuit.

In fact, while the lawsuit was pending, and regardless of how settlement discussions were going, Maize and Corning should have invited any Waterside residents who experienced any dissatisfaction with their MochaJava experiences to call the owners personally. And they should have made things right for all of those customers.

The same goes for the national companies that were dragged into the lawsuit later. Let's say one of those companies was Burger Village. A nationwide survey concludes that lots of Burger Village customers are unhappy about poor service, although there is no pattern related to race or national origin. Without admitting to any violation of non-discrimination laws, Burger Village's headquarters should make a commitment to reinforce its non-discrimination policies and to improve customer service generally. Burger Village should institute a "mystery diner" program to ensure that customers of all races receive comparable, excellent service. Burger Village should set up a toll-free number for customers to call if they have complaints about service at any company-owned or franchised restaurant. Customers with legitimate complaints should be offered refunds or complimentary meals. Burger Village might even institute a satisfaction guarantee.

The lesson here is that it's not uncommon for a customer service business to be accused of discrimination when in fact the bad service was not motivated by discrimination. In such a case, the business should apologize for poor service (note: not discriminatory service) and promise to correct the situation. And then do so. After that, the media are unlikely to be interested. There's no story.

In short, a customer service company which finds itself on the receiving end of a customer class action discrimination case should take responsibility for improving its customer service performance, which will help restore and maintain the trust of all of its customers. Taking this accountable approach, instead of denying a problem or trying to shift blame, defuses the neutron bomb before it detonates.

CHAPTER 3—NO WHITE COLLAR FOR HER

**Omni Supermarkets' Female Cashiers Denied
Promotions to Management; Union Campaign Intensifies**

Omni Supermarkets was the most profitable grocery chain in the mid-Atlantic region, with almost 400 stores. Omni's general manager, Pete Petrakis, carefully scouted for locations in communities with lots of unemployed housewives, who would accept part-time, minimum wage jobs without health care benefits. Petrakis avoided urban centers. While Omni's competitors may have set prices higher and done more volume per square foot in their city stores, Petrakis preferred the suburbs and even the "exurbs" where steady jobs were scarce and employees loyal. Every year, when Omni's competitors' union contracts expired and they were faced with strikes, Petrakis just chuckled. The unions never had won an election at an Omni store. Omni employees rarely even signed enough union cards to force an election.

Petrakis was proud of Omni's record of equal employment opportunity. The stores were careful to hire minorities in proportion to the population they served, and some African Americans and Hispanics had been promoted to store manager and division positions. Omni purchased produce and dairy goods locally, and Petrakis made sure that a substantial share of Omni's local procurement contracts went to minority vendors. Petrakis had accepted several awards from minority business associations and the Black Chamber of Commerce.

Omni's success posed a serious threat to the Affiliated Grocery Workers Union (AGWU). Omni's non-union operations were stealing market share from the unionized competition, resulting in a reduction in the number of AGWU-represented employees in the industry (and a corresponding drop in dues revenues). Perhaps more significant for the long term, as those traditionally unionized grocery companies opened new stores, their management was starting to resist union recognition, forcing elections which the union sometimes lost. In some markets where Omni had been growing quickly at its competitors' expense, employees of the unionized competitors had circulated decertification petitions. No AGWU-represented bargaining units had been decertified yet, but it was just a matter of time. In short, Omni was becoming the "bad boy" labor relations role model for the industry, and AGWU's survival was at risk.

The AGWU organizing committee decided that if Omni wouldn't cooperate with the union, the union would put Omni out of business. That would send the right message to Omni's competitors. At first, Omni tried "area standards" picketing of Omni stores—carrying signs advising the public that Omni didn't pay the wages and benefits common for the locality. Omni's customers didn't seem to care; very few took their business elsewhere. And Omni ran full-page ads in the local newspapers showing that their wage rates and benefits for full-time employees were comparable to (or higher than) the unionized competition. AGWU's pickets and handbills tried to explain that most of Omni's employees were part-timers, earning about half the hourly rate of full time workers and no health benefits—but the details were lost on the public and Omni seemed unperturbed by AGWU's "area standards" campaign.

Following the example of other AFL-CIO unions in their disputes with employers, AGWU mounted a full "corporate campaign" against Omni. AGWU urged a consumer boycott of Omni nationwide, but the general public didn't respond. Apparently even members of other AFL-CIO unions and their families didn't support the boycott, because there was no decline in the number of cars parked in Omni's parking lots—AGWU's own measure of the impact of the attempted boycott.

In fear of a total rout, AGWU focused on shifting Omni's stance from anti-union to "neutral." AGWU told Pete Petrakis the union would call a halt to its "corporate campaign" if Omni would do just two things: permit paid union organizers to solicit union support during non-working hours in Omni's parking lots, and recognize AGWU if the union obtained signed union cards from a majority of a store's employees. Petrakis flatly refused. Through advertisements and a letter-writing campaign, AGWU tried to get Omni's institutional and individual shareholders to support their demands for "neutrality," but no significant support was forthcoming.

A disgruntled former employee of an Omni store's meat department told an AGWU organizer about alleged problems with the way Omni handled meat and poultry. The employee claimed to have proof that out-dated meat and poultry products were re-labeled to allow them to be sold. The employee also claimed that Omni headquarters was aware of and even encouraged such deception. AGWU then got one of the national television networks to do an expose of Omni's food-handling practices at three stores, painting a picture of a company that put profits ahead of consumer safety. For three months, Omni's sales dropped, but after the same network exposed similar practices at Omni's major competitor, the buying public apparently dismissed the safety concerns as exaggerated (or at least, as having been remedied—or perhaps as being inevitable). Sales gradually returned to prior levels.

Throughout the corporate campaign, Pete Petrakis was able to keep Omni's management from panicking and giving in to AGWU. He was proud.

Sandi Schwartz, the chairperson of AGWU's organizing committee, finally concluded that Omni was immune to the "corporate campaign" tactics that had been so successful against other employers. Schwartz decided to get back to basics: How could the union prove its value to Omni's employees? Schwartz convened a meeting of officers of AGWU locals in the Mid-Atlantic States. In a brainstorming session, Schwartz called upon these Local officers to identify issues around which AGWU could rally support for the union among Omni's employees. At first glance, wages and benefits seemed like non-starters, given Omni's practice of meeting the compensation package of its competitors. But a couple of AGWU's local officers had a different perspective: Omni employed relatively few full-time employees; most Omni workers were part-timers earning minimum wage with no benefits. Employees who asked for full-time schedules were told that only part-time work was available. If they wanted full-time work, they left to work for competitors. Schwartz had her rallying cry: "Vote Union for full-time work, fair pay and benefits!"

It turned out that the vast majority of the Omni workers with part-time schedules (typically, the checkers) did not want full-time work. They were self-described "housewives" who needed to work part-time but had too many family obligations to work full time. The lack of benefits wasn't broadly perceived as a problem, because many of these women had husbands working full-time—and earning family benefits—elsewhere. The few who weren't satisfied with part-time work simply moved laterally to Omni's competitors, who were happy to hire trained and experienced grocery workers.

In other words, Omni's female employees knew that if and when they wanted full-time work, they could easily switch to other grocery stores. They weren't interested in fighting Omni, and they weren't interested in a union. Sandi Schwartz hadn't done enough homework. AGWU couldn't collect enough signatures on union cards to force an election at even a single Omni store.

In the course of developing this unsuccessful strategy to organize Omni, Schwartz had met several women who had left Omni due to unavailability of full-time work and had gone on to become AGWU officials at other grocery companies. In further discussions with these women, Schwartz learned something else: they had been motivated to leave Omni not only by the unavailability of full-time work, but by their belief that there was no chance of advancement at Omni because management jobs were reserved for men.

Schwartz did more research. She had representatives from the AGWU Locals in the Mid-Atlantic States drop by their local Omni stores and take a count of the gender profile of the store staff. Knowing the grocery business, these sleuths had no difficulty identifying the various department managers, day and night store managers, and others in the hierarchy of Omni's management. Although AGWU Local representatives visited only about one third of Omni's stores, the sample was large enough to be reliable and the results were astounding. No Omni store had a woman manager. Only a handful had a woman as a night manager or assistant manager. Almost no Omni stores had a female meat department manager or produce manager—the typical stepping-stones to store management positions.

In the grocery industry generally, women were under-represented in management positions; however, the disparity for Omni was much more substantial than for its competitors. Finally, Schwartz had an issue that would resonate with employees as well as the public: Omni discriminated against its female employees by steering them into part-time dead-end checker positions, while steering men into full-time positions in departments with upward mobility.

The AGWU International and several of the AGWU Local officials who were former Omni employees brought a class action lawsuit against Omni alleging that the chain discriminated against over 100,000 current and former female employees. In pre-trial discovery, AGWU learned that Omni's male entry-level employees (predominantly stockers) were 90% likely to be in full-time positions, while only 15% of Omni's female employees (predominantly checkers) were in full-time positions. As a practical matter, only full-time employees were eligible for promotion. Omni's baggers—most of whom were men—were promoted at rates exceeding the promotion rate of checkers, even though checker was a higher-paid position that required classroom training. To be a store manager required prior experience as a night manager or manager of a major department (such as the meat or produce department)—jobs with demanding schedules that Omni's incumbent female employees rarely were willing to take, even if offered.

In short, Omni had set up a self-perpetuating cycle of women being hired into checker jobs, at which they worked part-time for low compensation, with no reasonable expectation of career advancement. Ambitious women simply left Omni for a competitor and worked their way up through that company's ranks. Until AGWU sponsored the suit against Omni, no woman had gone to the expense and difficulty of pursuing a gender bias claim against Omni over this lack of opportunity. It simply wasn't worth it to any one woman, who could leave Omni and pursue her career ambitions with a competitor.

While the lawsuit was in pre-trial discovery, scores of women—current and former Omni employees—came forward with their allegations of discrimination. The typical story was of a checker who had trained male coworkers, only to see those less-qualified and less-experienced men get promoted over them. Many of these claims were barred by the statute of limitations from being raised in court; and Omni had other substantial defenses to almost all of the claims. For example, many of the men hired as baggers or stockers had college degrees in business, and Omni recruited them with the promise of moving them up to management positions after they gained some experience in a store. But those explanations were too complicated for a sound bite on the evening news. The publicity was overwhelmingly adverse. AGWU called for women to boycott Omni because of the way it treated female employees.

Unlike the previous boycott effort over wages and benefits, which had elicited only yawns, this one struck a resonant chord with women across the nation's socio-economic and political spectra. Shopping at a different grocery store was a small sacrifice to avenge decades of male domination in the workplace. Omni's financial results suffered and it began temporary layoffs—starting with the part-time checkers. In almost half of Omni's stores, the employees (including the laid-off checkers who still were considered "employees" under the labor law) overwhelmingly signed union cards and voted "For" AGWU in the elections, which followed.

So Pete Petrakis, whose careful attention to workforce demographics had made Omni exceedingly profitable for decades, wound up having to explain to Omni's CEO why they needed to spend $120 million to settle a sex discrimination case—and another $50 million per year for union-negotiated fringe benefits for employees at the stores where AGWU had won representation rights. Petrakis also had to explain that in those stores where the union had won recognition, Omni no longer could discipline or discharge employees for violations of work rules without exposing the company to the grievance and arbitration provisions of the AGWU contract.

To settle the lawsuit, Omni also had to agree to the court's appointment of a monitor to review all promotions for five years. Omni even had to commit to promote qualified women in proportion to their representation in entry-level positions, without regard to the part-time status of those entry positions, and without requiring rotation through the meat or produce department or the night shift.

Pete Petrakis retired from Omni.

What lesson can other employers learn from Omni's experience? That discrimination complaints aren't always raised by the victim. Third parties with an "agenda" can motivate, support—and even finance—class action discrimination cases. What should Omni have done to prevent this liability?

PROACTIVE STEPS TO DETER OUTSIDERS FROM

ENCOURAGING BIAS SUITS

- Conduct internal audits of vulnerability to bias suits.

- Establish and maintain an effective process for internal resolution of discrimination complaints, inform employees of the process and encourage them to use it.

- Be wary of any competitive advantages in labor costs.

- Get diverse views on the existence and extent of discrimination in the company.

- Know your adversaries.

- Don't put Operations people in charge of Human Resources.

First of all, don't assume that you'll have warning of a class action discrimination suit. Even if your company has few bias complaints, there may be disgruntled employees or former employees who are just waiting for the opportunity to sue you—particularly if someone else takes the initiative and provides the legal representation.

So, even if your employees aren't complaining of discrimination, you still should conduct routine internal audits of your employment practices to determine your vulnerability to bias suits. At least twice a year, for each establishment (factory, sales district, etc.), you should examine the impact of your hiring, promotion, compensation, discipline and discharge practices on protected groups. Don't focus solely on race. Also look at gender and age. Of course, there are other protected characteristics—national origin, religion, disability, and others. However, these characteristics aren't always (usually?) apparent, and it's generally wrong—and sometimes illegal—to ask. On the other hand, to the extent an employee has self-identified as having a disability or requiring a religious accommodation, someone with Human Resources responsibility should be monitoring to ensure compliance with applicable legal requirements.

If you find that a particular employment practice has a disparate impact on a protected group (for example, if your standardized test for promotions to management screens out African Americans at a rate significantly higher than it screens out whites), this does not mean that you are guilty of discrimination. A practice with disparate impact is lawful if the employer can establish business necessity (job-related-ness) of the practice. For example, a validation study performed by an industrial psychologist may justify use of a standardized test that has a significantly lower pass rate for African Americans.

Even though the existence of disparate impact doesn't mean a law has been broken, it does increase the likelihood of a challenge because, by definition, there is an affected class of "victims" of the practice. And, as demonstrated by the hypothetical cases discussed in these first three chapters (and the real life cases on which they are based), public opinion usually focuses on the victims, not the justification for the different treatment or outcome. Public opinion often forces companies to settle discrimination cases, which could have been defended, successfully in the courts (or at least to pay more in settlement than the actuarial estimate of the loss in litigation).

So Omni's first mistake was its ignorance of the lack of career opportunities for women. Even though Pete Petrakis was well aware that women typically were hired into part-time dead-end positions, Petrakis did not identify this as a potential problem for Omni, and therefore did not bring it to the attention of higher management. Meanwhile, upwardly mobile women left Omni every day to work for competitors. Although some of them told their immediate bosses that their reason for changing jobs was to take higher-paid positions, no one thought this was significant information to communicate to higher levels.

If Omni had established and maintained an effective process for internal resolution of discrimination complaints, and had informed employees of the process and encouraged them to use it, Omni probably would have learned years earlier of the discontent of female employees who aspired to careers (not just part-time jobs) in the grocery business.

Pete Petrakis was proud of Omni's competitive advantage in labor costs. It didn't occur to him that the "savings" Omni enjoyed reflected the poor bargaining power of women seeking entry-level part-time positions. The "free market" allowed Omni to pay these women less than Omni's competitors paid their full time workers under union contracts. However, during the pretrial discovery in the AGWU case, it became apparent that Omni matched its unionized competitors' compensation for full-time cashiers, stockers, baggers, and a host of other positions. So Omni's labor cost advantage was attributable entirely to the lower pay of Omni's part-time cashiers, almost all of who were women. This gave AGWU the opening it needed. Disgruntled employees (or former employees) will seek revenge when given the opportunity.

Another reason Omni didn't see the class action coming was that its leadership consisted entirely of men. When Pete Petrakis made his quarterly presentations to the management committee and bragged about Omni's low cost of sales, he took credit for having selected sites with an abundance of "housewives" who were "happy to work for the minimum wage." If a woman sat on Omni's management committee, it's likely that she would have asked Petrakis a question or two about those women and whether they really wanted—and would be satisfied with—dead-end entry-level jobs.

There were women in Omni's general management, but they weren't integrated into the informal "good old boy" network. Unlike their male counterparts, the women never were invited to play golf with Omni's senior managers, or to go out for a drink with "the boys" after work. They were excluded from a variety of other informal get-togethers where business was discussed (and careers built). As a result, Omni's leadership lost numerous opportunities for valuable sharing of points of view.

Once again, the key to minimizing the risk of discrimination law-suits is to attract, retain and advance a diverse workforce at all levels of the business, and consistently to seek input from employees of diverse backgrounds on whether discriminatory practices exist in the company. Obviously, every company will have among its employees some malcontents. It's impossible to satisfy everyone, and it would be foolish to solicit advice from every employee. Still, at every level of the business there are employees who are known to be loyal, hardworking and effective. If those employees represent diverse perspectives, their opinions on employee relations issues should be sought and seriously considered. It would have been a simple, and productive, exercise for Pete Petrakis to have asked a female store manager whether she thought Omni was doing a good job attracting, retaining and advancing women in the business.

Perhaps the worst human resources mistake Omni made was to assume it had no adversaries on human resources issues. In the marketing arena, Omni spent hundreds of thousands of dollars a year on so-called competitive intelligence to predict what moves its competitors would make, and how its competitors would react to Omni's initiatives. If Omni offered customers double the value of cents-off coupons, would the competitors follow? How soon? If Omni stopped offering to double coupons, by how much would gross sales fall before the competition also stopped doubling? Omni had a vice president of marketing whose entire job responsibility was to predict and make contingency plans for competition.

Yet, in the human resources area, Omni didn't even know it had adversaries, much less who those adversaries were. If pressed, Omni's vice president for human resources would have identified a handful of employees—"troublemakers"—as adversaries. While it was common knowledge that AGWU wanted to organize Omni's workers, the Union's track record in elections was so consistently bad that no one in Omni's top management took the union threat seriously. Even when

AGWU got the network news media interested in safety issues, Omni's public relations department fought back with an effective campaign that had been planned well in advance, in anticipation of one or another food poisoning catastrophe.

But no one at Omni imagined that the union which had failed to organize the employees in any Omni store would become their champion in litigation over promotions to management—promotions to jobs which weren't even in the bargaining unit and which therefore didn't affect AGWU's dues revenues. What Omni overlooked is that an adversary can attack any vulnerability to weaken its opponent. AGWU didn't really care whether checkers got promoted to store manager positions, but AGWU used that issue to build commitment to the union movement and to AGWU in particular. In short, AGWU got Omni's predominantly female workforce to take sides with AGWU in its battle with Omni, tipping the scales decidedly in AGWU's favor. The lesson here is to identify your adversaries and think a step ahead of their planning. Competitors, unions, terminated executives—all of these and others can be the instigators of discrimination lawsuits.

Omni's final and fatal mistake was that it allowed Pete Petrakis, general manager, to make decisions that ought to have been made by (or, at least, with the concurrence of) a human resources professional. It was natural for Omni to empower Petrakis to select sites for new stores. Petrakis had been with Omni for over 20 years and he had demonstrated time and again that he could pick profitable locations. But as soon as Omni's management committee started hearing Petrakis brag about "housewives eager to earn the minimum wage, with no health benefits," they should have involved Omni's vice president for human resources, to determine whether Petrakis' assumptions were sound and whether Petrakis' proposed approach was good business.

Any experienced human resources professional would have seen the disastrous long-run implications of segregating the workforce into a predominantly female group working part-time with no advancement, and a predominantly male group working full time at substantially higher pay and with a predictable career path. If Omni's actual vice president of human resources had been more proactive, he would have conducted periodic risk assessments ("Where's our next lawsuit likely to come from?")—and he would have determined that Petrakis' method of operating posed too much danger to the company. Instead, Omni's human resources vice president did what he had been hired to do, which was to oversee a department of personnel managers who processed personnel transactions (recruitment, hiring, performance evaluation, compensation, discipline, separation). Omni didn't encourage its human resources vice president to participate in corporate strategic planning, so he didn't. After the class action was settled, the human resources vice president was replaced by an "activist."

II. HOW TO PREVENT DISCRIMINATION CLAIMS

Chapter 4—How To Adopt, Impement And Enforce A "Zero Tolerance" Non-Discrimination Policy

Every business should have a policy prohibiting all forms of unlawful discrimination and specifying how allegations of discrimination will be investigated and resolved. Such a written policy is practically required to meet legal obligations. Even more important, publishing such a policy is a prominent statement that your company operates on a highly ethical basis. Whatever your company's vision and mission statements may say about your other business objectives, be sure to include a commitment to fair treatment of your employees. Your detailed policy on equal employment opportunity should refer back to your vision or mission statement, reinforcing that fair treatment of your employees is one of your core values.

The CEO should sign the policy, and if the business has more than one location or establishment, the highest-ranking official in the location or establishment also should sign. The policy should be posted prominently on employee bulletin boards and should be reviewed with every employee at the time of hire and annually thereafter.

Employees should be required to sign an acknowledgment that they have read the policy, that they understand it, and that they agree to be bound by it. Any employee who refuses to sign should be terminated—even the top salesperson or an executive. The non-discrimination policy of a retail business should include a commitment to the unbiased treatment of customers, as well as procedures for impartial review of customer complaints of discrimination. Any customer who complains of discrimination should be given a copy of the policy.

The content of a non-discrimination policy necessarily will vary from business to business, but there are several essential elements: the types of conduct prohibited, the procedures for resolving claims of discrimination, and the consequences of violating the policy.

A NON-DISCRIMINATION POLICY SHOULD ANSWER THE FOLLOWING QUESTIONS:

- What types of conduct are prohibited?
- What are the procedures for resolving a claim of discrimination?
- What are the consequences of a finding of discrimination?

It is just as important that the policy avoid making gratuitous promises, which may be difficult (or even impossible) to keep.

A NON-DISCRIMINATION POLICY SHOULD AVOID MAKING ANY OF THE FOLLOWING PROMISES:

- All reports of suspected discrimination will be kept strictly confidential.
- All employees are promised a harassment-free workplace.
- All employees will be treated fairly.

Why not promise employees that their discrimination complaints will be kept confidential? Because, in the course of investigating the alleged discrimination, the investigator will have to talk to all of the witnesses, including the alleged perpetrator. In some cases, the victim and the perpetrator were alone, so the perpetrator will know who made the report. Even if the investigator can avoid disclosing the informant, if the perpetrator is disciplined or discharged, and files a lawsuit or grievance, the company may have to call the informant as a witness. If the informant is someone other than the victim of the alleged discrimination, and the victim files a complaint with a government agency or court, the company may have to disclose the informant as part of its defense.

Why not promise employees a harassment-free workplace? Because some personality conflicts are inevitable. As long as the conflict is not related to race, gender, or some other "protected characteristic," employees may have to tolerate it. For example, a boss who refers to all of his subordinates as "lazy idiots" and screams at them to work faster may be "harassing" them, but this conduct is not discriminatory and is not prohibited by an equal employment opportunity policy.

Why not promise employees that they will be treated fairly? Because "fairness" is in the eye of the beholder. A boss who fires an employee for being late six times in a year may believe that the discharge is fair, but the employee may complain that the boss ignored the reasons for his tardiness and therefore acted unfairly.

Here is a model non-discrimination policy for a retail business:

TOUGH TOGS, INC.
POLICY PROHIBITING DISCRIMINATION

This policy is effective October 2000, and supersedes and replaces any prior policies on this subject. This policy applies to all Tough Togs, Inc. corporate offices and to all franchise locations in the United States.

Tough Togs, Inc. is committed to equal employment opportunity. Equal employment opportunity policies ensure that all employees and applicants for employment have the same opportunities for success and are provided a work environment free from unlawful discrimination.

It is the policy of Tough Togs, Inc. to provide equal opportunity in all aspects of the employment relationship, including the following:

Benefits	Layoff	Recruitment
Compensation	Leaves of absence	Social and recreational programs
Disciplinary actions	Promotions	Termination of employment
Hiring	Recall from layoff	Transfers

Conditions and privileges of employment are administered to all employees without unlawful discrimination because of the following "protected characteristics":

Age	Gender	Religion
Color	National origin	Sexual orientation
Disability	Race	Covered veteran status

Tough Togs, Inc.'s continuing commitment to a work environment free from unlawful discrimination is the responsibility of the entire work force. All Tough Togs, Inc. employees are accountable for compliance with this non-discrimination policy. As a condition of employment, every employee is expected to treat all other employees, customers, vendors and other business visitors fairly and equally. The involvement of each supervisor and manager in working to achieve the purpose of this policy will be reflected in his or her performance appraisal.

Harassment is one type of discrimination prohibited under this policy. Prohibited harassment includes sexually or racially degrading words used to describe an individual, comments or jokes of a sexist, ethnic, age-related or racial nature, and displaying sexually-suggestive objects or pictures or pictures which are derogatory of a person's ethnicity, age, race or gender. Sending a harassing message or picture by electronic means such as e-mail violates this policy whether the employee sending it was the originator or was forwarding something received from another person.

Examples of prohibited sexual harassment include unwelcome invitations, flirtations, physical contact (such as kissing, hugging, patting, pinching or brushing up against another person), advances, requests for sexual favors, propositions, or comments about an individual's body. Prohibited sexual harassment also includes any other conduct which tends to create a sexually hostile work environment or implies that employment, advancement, compensation, performance evaluation, assigned duties, shifts or any other term or condition of employment is dependent upon an employee's submission to sexual advances. Same-gender harassment (a man harassing a man or a woman harassing a woman) violates this policy whether or not such conduct is unlawful.

This policy also prohibits treating any customer, vendor or other business visitor differently because of that person's "protected characteristic." For example, no Tough Togs store will have check-cashing rules for minority customers unless the same rules apply to non-minority customers.

Any employee who believes that he or she has been subject to discrimination at work, or in any way related to his or her employment with Tough Togs, must make a report to Tough Togs' equal opportunity compliance office at 1-800-555-1234. Any employee who has observed or has been told about discrimination against any other Tough Togs employee, or against any Tough Togs customer, vendor or other business visitor must make a report to the equal opportunity compliance office at the number above. This obligation extends to situations where the person alleged to have committed the harassment is an outsider, such as a customer or vendor. Anonymous reports will be accepted.

Tough Togs, Inc. will not tolerate any activity that has a demeaning effect on any employee, customer, vendor or other business visitor. Any employee who violates this non-discrimination policy, whether by participating in discriminatory conduct or failing to report discriminatory conduct to the equal opportunity compliance office, will be subject to discipline up to and including discharge. Any supervisor or manager who fails to take appropriate disciplinary action against an employee who has been determined after an investigation to have violated this non-discrimination policy will be discharged.

Any customer, vendor or other business visitor who believes that a Tough Togs employee has subjected him or her to discrimination may file a complaint with Tough Togs' equal opportunity office by calling the number above.

Anyone who makes a report in good faith to the equal opportunity compliance office, or who cooperates with an investigation, will be protected from any adverse action for making the report or participating in the investigation. Any employee who retaliates against another employee, or against a customer, vendor or other business visitor, for reporting suspected discrimination or for participating in an investigation will be discharged immediately. Any employee who interferes with a compliance office investigation will be discharged immediately. Any employee who discloses anything about a compliance office investigation without the prior written permission of the compliance office will be discharged immediately. This includes statements to news media.

In addition to reporting alleged discrimination to the equal opportunity compliance office, complaints may be filed with the U.S. Equal Employment Opportunity Commission or in some locations, with a state or local fair-employment-practice agency.

Questions about this policy should be directed to your supervisor or to the director of the equal opportunity compliance office at 1-800-555-1234.

_____   _____
    Chief Executive Officer   Local/Establishment Head

You might want to break up the text into smaller blocks and publish the policy as a brochure or booklet.

At the time of hire, and annually thereafter, each employee should be required to read the non-discrimination policy and to make a commitment to follow the policy. Each employee should be required to sign an acknowledgment, such as this:

Employee Acknowledgment:
I have read Tough Togs, Inc.'s Policy Prohibiting Discrimination dated October 2000. I was given sufficient time to ask questions about the policy. I understand the policy. I agree to comply with the policy.

_____   _____   __/__/__
Signature   Name (Printed)   Date

Once a company has adopted a nondiscrimination policy and all employees have agreed to follow the policy, the company must enforce it rigorously. Chapter 6 of this book describes in detail how to conduct an effective and credible investigation of a discrimination complaint. Chapter 8 discusses how to remedy actual and perceived discrimination, while building trust with customers, investors, employees and other stakeholders.

Assuming that an investigation confirms that a company employee engaged in discriminatory conduct, what is the appropriate penalty? Even if the employee previously had a perfect work record, some offenses warrant immediate discharge:

- unwelcome sexual touching
- conditioning promotion, wages, or any other condition of employment on sexual favors
- making an adverse employment decision based upon another employee's protected characteristic (such as firing the oldest cashier)

By way of contrast, here are some examples of offenses which are serious but which do not necessarily require immediate discharge (unless there were aggravating circumstances or prior incidents):

- telling a sexist or racist joke (although use of the "n" word or similar epithets probably should result in immediate discharge)
- asking a coworker for a date after the coworker made it clear that he or she was not interested
- displaying a sexually-suggestive picture at work

In cases like these, discipline short of discharge may be imposed. The higher the position of the employee, the more severe the discipline should be. Here is a range of possible penalties:

- demotion
- pay cut
- denial of raise and/or bonus
- written reprimand

Regardless of the penalty imposed, the employee must be warned that any subsequent violation of the non-discrimination policy will result in immediate discharge. This warning must be recorded in the employee's personnel file, and it is helpful (although not essential) to have the employee sign an acknowledgment.

Exceptions must not be permitted for employees who are otherwise considered essential. Often, transgressions by top salespeople or by executives are overlooked, or it is assumed that the offender will "get the message" and not repeat the violation. This is a dangerous approach. If the top salesman in a company had lit a fire in the warehouse, or a vice president had sold a secret to a competitor, he would be fired on the spot. No one would suggest just withholding the salesman's bonus for a quarter or "coaching" the vice president. To treat discriminatory conduct less severely is foolhardy. A sexual harassment case easily can cost the business more than an act of arson or industrial espionage!

Notwithstanding the requirement that employees report suspected discrimination to a compliance office or another official, employees often don't file such complaints. Why? Some employees are afraid of retaliation, regardless of written policies prohibiting such adverse actions. Other employees believe that they can correct the discrimination themselves. To ensure that discrimination is being surfaced and corrected, periodic audits must be conducted. These audits are most effective if conducted by someone experienced in equal opportunity principles, but a district or division manager who oversees other business issues certainly can be trained to review compliance with the nondiscrimination policy as well.

In addition to helping you avoid lawsuits, a rigorous non-discrimination policy, enforced vigorously, will help your company achieve the status of "employer of choice." Good people want to work for a company that protects its employees from harassing and otherwise discriminatory conduct. Customers want to buy from a company that has a reputation for being a good place to work. It's smart business.

Chapter 5—What Is "Diversity" And What Kind Of "Diversity Management" Policy Is Right For Your Company

What is "diversity" and how is it different from equal employment opportunity? "Diversity" means differences. Men and women are different. Blacks and whites are different. Young people and seniors are different. Gays and straight people are different. People from the South are different from Midwesterners. Catholics are different from Protestants.

Various laws require companies to have policies prohibiting discrimination in employment. And federal government contractors are required to have "affirmative action programs" encouraging the hiring and advancement of women, minorities, qualified individuals with disabilities and certain veterans. Full compliance with these laws and regulations does not mean that a company's workforce will match the demographics of the community, however.

For example, the population of Waterside may be 20 percent Hispanic. Yet, if the Waterside MochaJava restaurant advertises an opening for an experienced manager, the pool of applicants may or may not include Hispanics, depending on the availability of Hispanics with the requisite restaurant management experience and interest in the position. It is entirely possible that the MochaJava restaurant, without discriminating, will have no Hispanics on its management team.

Is that a problem? From a legal compliance standpoint, perhaps not. But a customer-driven business will be less effective, and ultimately less profitable, if its workforce fails to reflect the characteristics of its customer base. Even if the Waterside MochaJava restaurant had few Hispanic customers, a Hispanic manager might conceive of ways to reach that market segment—perhaps some additional menu offerings (Cuban style coffee?) or promotions (coupons in the Latino newspaper).

At the highest levels of business—senior officers and the Board of Directors—having diverse perspectives is essential to business survival and growth. If strategic moves such as mergers, new products, and appointments of executives are decided by middle-aged, straight, Anglo Saxon men without the balance of other points of view, suboptimal decisions are likely.

For example, if a certain brewery company had a Native American on its senior management staff or its Board of Directors, it probably would not have made the mistake of naming a new malt liquor after a revered Indian chief. If automobile manufacturers had Hispanics in important marketing positions, they probably would not have named an automobile "Matador" (which translates as "killer" in Spanish) or "Nova" (which means "doesn't go"). If a certain furniture manufacturer *didn't* have gay employees in influential jobs, it might never have run what turned out to be a very successful television ad campaign pitched ever so subtly toward gay couples.

"Diversity management" is the term given to a corporate policy of maximizing the contribution of the company's diverse human resources. It is impossible to provide a precise definition of "diversity management" because every business must develop its own. However, here are some essential elements:

ESSENTIAL ELEMENTS OF A DIVERSITY POLICY

- Peoples' differences—race, gender, age, ethnicity, sexual preference, etc.—will be respected.

- Differing points of view are welcome when a problem is being addressed. Accordingly, whenever possible, employee teams will include individuals of varying personal characteristics; however, once a course of action has been decided, everyone will support the decision.

- Despite their differences, all employees will be held to the same performance standards.

- To the extent feasible, a diverse team of selectors will make hiring and promotion decisions.

- When customer opinions are being solicited, individuals of diverse backgrounds will be included.

- When products or services are being advertised, models of diverse backgrounds will be featured and diverse media will be used.

It's equally important to leave *out* of a company's diversity policy promises that cannot, or should not, be kept.

PROMISES TO AVOID IN A DIVERSITY POLICY

- At all levels of the business, women and minorities will be employed in proportion to their representation in the community.

- People's differences are to be celebrated.

Why not promise to employ women and minorities in proportion to their representation in the community? The problem here is that women and minorities with the qualifications for and interest in particular jobs may be "available" at rates differing from the general population. For example, women may constitute 51% of the population of Waterside, but only 5% of the skilled construction workers in Waterside may be women. A construction firm would have an impossible time trying to hire as many women as men for skilled construction jobs. Another problem with setting rigid goals for minority and female employment is that non-minorities and men may successfully challenge such a policy as an impermissible "quota."

Why not promise to celebrate people's differences? Because it's enough to respect differences without requiring employees to endorse each other's lifestyles. For example, a conservative company shouldn't derogate its gay employees' sexual preference, but there is no need to celebrate Gay Pride Day if doing so would offend the vast majority of the employee body, including evangelical Christians. It's enough to respect the gay lifestyle without promoting it.

Putting this into practice, usually a "diversity management" program has two major thrusts: (a) developing a workforce that reflects (without necessarily matching) the diversity of the company's customers and other stakeholders, such as legislators, regulators, investors and community groups; and (b) creating and maintaining a work environment where each employee is able to achieve his or her full potential, capitalizing on the individual attributes of each individual.

Some companies have rushed to embrace "diversity management" in silly and self-defeating ways. One large company sponsored an ethnic event each week, like a polka party to celebrate the employees of Polish heritage, which served only to trivialize the "diversity" concept. Another company put on a series of seminars designed to confront hidden biases by subjecting every employee to racist or ethnic epithets. Of course, the result was a tremendous increase in hostility and polarization of the workforce along racial and ethnic lines.

Another company imposed strict hiring and promotion quotas in an effort to mirror the population of the community in which the company was located. This led to "reverse" discrimination lawsuits and a perception that the women and minorities did not deserve their jobs.

So what's the right way to go about "diversity management"? First, recognize that the key concepts are *inclusiveness* and *respect*. When hiring, promoting, forming special project teams, and conducting other important business affairs, *include* people of diverse backgrounds and interests. When working with people different from ourselves, *respect* each individual for his or her contributions, even if he or she has a different outlook, approach or style.

Let's get down to details. If mostly people of homogeneous backgrounds presently populate your company, how can you increase the diversity of your workforce while maintaining high standards and not alienating the existing employees?

At the highest levels (Board of Directors and senior management), no selection should be made unless the slate of candidates is "diverse," meaning that the slate includes at least one well-qualified woman and one well-qualified minority. Sometimes, this may mean looking outside the company. If search firms are used, their contracts should require them to present diverse slates of qualified candidates. If the company is large enough to have a succession planning process, women and minorities, seniors, gays, and all other "groups" should be well represented.

Even at lower levels, emphasis should be placed on *including* people of diverse backgrounds when selecting applicants for hire or employees for promotion. And whenever possible, the selections should be made by two or more selectors—of diverse backgrounds. It's just too easy for Protestant white men to find other Protestant white men "best qualified" for jobs.

Assuming you already have a diverse workforce, or you achieve that diversity, how do you derive value for your company from that diversity? How do you get those diverse employees to make their maximum contributions to problem solving? How do you get them to express their creative ideas? Obviously, you have to make all of the team members feel that they are valued. If some employees believe they are not valued because other employees hold stereotyped ideas about race, gender or other characteristics, they will not feel empowered and will not work to their fullest potential.

Employees need to be educated to treat each other with *respect*, as individuals, and to avoid stereotypical thinking. One-day seminars can be very helpful in pointing out how natural it is to stereotype and how communication and collaboration are limited by stereotypes. In such a seminar, participants explore cultural differences by examining their own values and assumptions—and then they work on seeing issues from other points of view.

Upper management has to set the tone in everything they do. For example, senior managers should not set important company events to coincide with the Jewish Day of Atonement, Yom Kippur. At the beginning of each year, a high official should circulate a calendar listing all significant religious holidays, with an admonition not to schedule team meetings on those days. Employees who want to take Martin Luther King's birthday off should be allowed to take a vacation day— no questions asked. No company official should use any kind of race- or sex-based joke in any setting. Employees' performance appraisals must include "diversity management" as an element. For lower level employees, the requirement would be to attend the training and to treat coworkers with respect for differences. For higher-level employees, the objective would be to take proactive steps to enhance interpersonal relationships in the workplace. All of these steps demonstrate that employees of diverse backgrounds and interests are *respected*.

A common barrier to the advancement of women and minorities is a lack of mentoring. In American companies, the senior managers tend to be white men. They tend to feel most comfortable around other white men, and they may see a bit of themselves in white male subordinates. It's only natural for bosses to offer career advice and guidance to subordinates with whom they feel "connected." Conversely, the shortage of women and minorities at higher levels in a company makes it less likely that women and minorities at lower levels will be mentored. In short, the "good old boy" network perpetuates itself even in the absence of intentional bias.

To break this pattern, every senior manager must make a point of knowing the promising women and minorities in his or her organization, going down several levels, and must take personal responsibility for ensuring that these subordinates get opportunities to advance—training, developmental assignments, task forces—whatever it takes in that company to get ahead. This mentoring must occur separate and apart from any formal program like succession planning, and must not be bureaucratic. Any senior manager should be able to name the high-potential women and minorities in that organization (as well as the high-potential white men), and the senior manager should be able to talk about the last time he or she checked on their progress and opportunities. This leadership sets the tone for managers at all levels of the business to engage in the same kind of mentoring.

Mentoring works best when it is accomplished without publishing detailed policies and procedures. If the CEO is the role model and ensures that his or her direct reports follow his lead, the behavior will manifest itself throughout the company.

Mentoring alone is not enough to ensure equal opportunity for advancement. It's also important to ensure equal access to career-advancing training, transfers and other developmental assignments (such as task forces, international assignments or special project teams). Otherwise, the "glass ceiling" may block the advancement of qualified women and minorities. If the company has a centralized human resources staff, someone in that organization could be given the responsibility for tracking all training, transfers and developmental assignments to ensure that there is no disparate impact against protected groups and to recommend specific courses, moves or assignments for "high potential" employees.

To ensure that equal employment opportunity and diversity management policies are being followed, periodic audits should be conducted. Ideally, every establishment or business unit would be audited every two years. (If there were a Department of Labor audit of an establishment, an internal audit would not be required until two years later.) When an internal audit is conducted, the head of the establishment or business unit being audited should be required to participate (with a minimum time commitment of two hours).

The most effective audit team will include insiders as well as at least one impartial, outside auditor. In a large company, one or more full-time internal auditors could move from establishment to establishment, teaming up with Human Resources heads from other establishments. This would provide the required person-power to conduct the audits while educating the Human Resources heads to diversity issues.

The fact that audits are being conducted should not be a secret. In fact, employee awareness of ongoing audits and action plans devolving from those audits strengthens employee confidence in the company's commitment to equal employment opportunity.

Audit reports should be limited to the action items, which the establishment or business unit has agreed to take. The report can be worded in positive terms without any admissions of liability and the results shared with senior management and the Board of Directors (or an appropriate committee of the Board). Satisfaction of the action items should also be reported to senior management and the Board. Audit reports should not be shared with employees generally, although action items should be discussed with the employees affected.

Avoiding discrimination and eliminating artificial barriers to employees' full participation and advancement won't automatically translate into higher profits. You still have to leverage the diversity of your workforce.

For example, how can having a diverse workforce expand your sales? As you consider market niches, segments, targeted products, and other strategies, be sure to *include* employees of diverse backgrounds and interests in the decision-making process. They may be able to identify customer groups you hadn't previously considered. For example, an employee in her sixties might identify the potential for selling a sports/health beverage to physically-fit seniors. An Asian employee might suggest an advertising campaign for a bank that appeals to traditional Asian values. Hispanic employees could join Latino community groups and use those contacts to develop support for the company's proposal to rezone property for a factory.

The manager in charge of advertising should make sure that customers of diverse backgrounds and interests are featured in advertising, and that diverse advertising media are utilized (for example, running print ads in the city's "alternative" paper as well as the mainstream daily).

Some companies find it useful to establish one or more "diversity councils," which meet periodically to discuss the company's successes and challenges in the area of "diversity management." In some corporate cultures, the results are positive. In others, the diversity council becomes a monthly bitching session. It might be a good idea to try out such a council for a month or two before committing significant resources.

The most effective "diversity management" programs are those which become so fully incorporated in the company's daily business that employees of all backgrounds and interests feel *respected*, diverse employees are *included* in every aspect of the company's operations, and no one has the title "diversity manager."

III. HOW TO SURVIVE DISCRIMINATION CLAIMS

Chapter 6—How To Conduct An Effective And Credible Investigation Of A Discrimination Complaint

Every company should have a process for investigating and resolving employment discrimination complaints before they grow into lawsuits. The same process can be extended to complaints of discrimination brought by customers or suppliers. Investigations help to identify problems at early stages, when corrective action is relatively easy and inexpensive. In addition, the existence of a thorough investigatory procedure for discrimination claims reinforces your company's core values of integrity, respect and fair dealing, thereby helping you to achieve "employer of choice" status. This chapter provides the blueprint for an effective complaint investigation process.

The first issue is *who should receive complaints* of discrimination. Clearly, employees should not have to report their claims to the alleged perpetrator. Because employment discrimination complaints often arise from the boss-subordinate relationship, employees must be provided an alternative person to whom they can complain. Anonymous complaints also should be accepted, although anonymous complainants should be told that by refusing to identify themselves, they might preclude a thorough investigation from being conducted.

A large company might establish a discrimination "hotline" telephone number, staffed by trained equal employment opportunity counselors. Ideally, such a staff would report to a corporate officer with responsibility for legal compliance. A smaller company might direct employees to contact the human resources or personnel department. Another option would be to contract out the function of receiving discrimination complaints to a vendor that would provide the "intake" function and refer appropriate cases for investigation.

Even if employees are instructed to report alleged discrimination to a particular person or group, as a legal matter the company is deemed to be aware of a complaint as soon as it is known by any member of management. Accordingly, every management employee should be instructed to report any claims of discrimination to the designated person or group. Every complaint should be logged in, and the final finding and action taken should be noted in the log.

The next question is *who should conduct the investigation*. The investigator may, but need not, be the same person to whom complaints are reported. To maintain impartiality, the investigator must not be in the chain of command of the complaining employee, any other alleged victim, or the alleged perpetrator. Ideally, the investigator would report to a senior officer of the company who would report (on these issues) directly to the Board of Directors. That way, alleged discrimination can be investigated internally no matter how high up in the company it arises. An alternative investigator would have to be appointed only in the event of a complaint involving someone in the investigator's own chain of command.

At the time this book is going to press, the Federal Trade Commission (FTC) has taken the position that any investigation conducted by a non-employee (such as a law firm or a company that specializes in investigations) must meet all of the requirements of an investigatory credit report under the Fair Credit Reporting Act. This includes obtaining *permission* from the target of the investigation and providing notices to the target of the investigation if adverse employment action is expected to result from the findings. Obviously, compliance with these requirements would compromise the investigation. The FTC supports federal legislation to carve out an exception for investigations of employee misconduct, including discrimination. In the meantime, you may want to have investigations conducted by an investigator on your payroll, who is not subject to these restrictions.

In any event, the investigator should have some training in basic equal employment law—at the very least, a two or three day course such as those which are conducted around the country by human resources organizations. The investigator should have some training or experience in auditing, interviewing or some other type of investigation. Detailed knowledge of equal employment opportunity law is less important than investigatory skill.

How should an investigation proceed? The first step in an investigation usually is to interview the complainant and the alleged victim(s) if the person filing the complaint isn't also the victim. Just as in journalism, the objective of this stage of the investigation is to determine the complainant's and/or victim's version of who did what to whom, when, and who witnessed the events. Even if the victim is reluctant, or asks the investigator not to pursue the issue, it is essential to conduct a thorough investigation. The company has a legal obligation to investigate alleged discrimination and recent U.S. Supreme Court cases make it clear that the adequacy of the action you take in response to internal complaints will be a significant factor in your defense to that claim and to other future claims. The victim should be assured of non-retaliation but must cooperate in the investigation.

While face-to-face interviews are preferable because it is easier to judge credibility in person, telephone interviews are acceptable for the initial fact gathering. The exception is if the complainant or victim insists upon a face-to-face meeting, in which case it could be counterproductive to require the investigation to proceed by telephone interview.

Every interview should begin with the investigator introducing himself or herself and promising the person being interviewed that there will be no retaliation for participating in the investigation. The investigator should instruct the interviewee not to discuss the fact that there is an investigation, or anything about the investigation, with anyone, including the interviewee's bosses or coworkers—even if they also have been interviewed. The investigator should emphasize that violation of the confidentiality of investigations will result in severe discipline, up to and including discharge. This is essential to prevent witnesses (or the alleged perpetrator) from being tipped off—and to prevent the rumor mill from spinning. At the same time, the investigator should not promise total confidentiality, for the reasons discussed in Chapter 4.

The investigator should take detailed notes (although tape recording is not recommended because it may intimidate witnesses). The investigator should pay particular attention to any inconsistencies in the story of the complainant or victim. Inconsistencies often indicate lack of truthfulness. In each interview, the investigator should ask the witness for back-up documentation, including notes, drawings, and e-mail messages. The investigator should also ask each witness to identify any other witnesses.

Until the investigation is complete, the investigator should not advise any witness as to the investigator's opinions or conclusions. The investigator should be careful not to give the impression of agreeing with the views of any witnesses until the investigation is finished. As other witnesses are interviewed and additional information is received, the investigator may change his or her mind.

After interviewing the complainant, the next step typically is to interview witnesses other than the alleged perpetrator and to collect and analyze any relevant data and documents. For example, if the case involves a woman's complaint that she deserved a promotion that went to a man, the investigator would collect statistics on promotions, by gender, in the complainant's organization; and if the selecting manager attributed the selection to the man's better record of performance, the investigator would review the performance evaluations of the man and the woman. If the woman's performance evaluation had been higher under previous bosses, the investigator would interview those bosses to determine whether the current evaluation was biased.

Generally, it's advisable to defer interviewing the alleged wrongdoer until all the other witnesses have told their stories, so that the investigator can "challenge" the alleged wrongdoer with any incriminating information. Often, it is necessary to circle back and re-interview complainants, victims and other witnesses as conflicting versions of events emerge.

Some investigations are easily resolved. For example, if the claim is one of gender discrimination against women in promotions, and the investigator finds that the female candidate lacked even the basic qualifications for the higher position, it may be possible to close out the investigation. A careful investigator would check to see whether the manager making the selection decision had a history of promoting only men (in which case his articulated reason for the current selection might be a pretext for discrimination).

Some investigations come down to credibility. Using the promotion example, perhaps both the woman and the man had the basic qualifications for the higher position. The selecting manager told the investigator that he picked the man because the man had five years of related work experience, while the woman had only two—although she also had a two-year college degree in the field. The investigator's task is not to decide whether a two-year college degree trumps three years of additional work experience; rather the investigator's job is to assess whether the selecting manager's articulated reason for preferring the male candidate is legitimate, nondiscriminatory, and genuine.

Resolution of credibility disputes is a judgment call. If the investigation has been thorough, the investigator will have documented reasons for believing one version of the events over others. Factors to consider when weighing credibility of each witness include the following: demeanor, consistency, any motive to lie, and any relevant prior history. The investigator should not dismiss a complaint as unfounded just because it comes down to one person's word against another's. In court, the burden of proof in a discrimination case is on the plaintiff, who must prove his or her case by a preponderance of the evidence, meaning that the plaintiff's version of the events is more likely than not what actually happened. A company should not hold a complaining employee to a higher standard of proof, such as the "beyond a reasonable doubt" test used in criminal prosecutions.

Once the investigation is complete, if the investigator concludes that discrimination did not occur, the investigator should so advise the complainant, any alleged victim other than the complainant, and the alleged perpetrator. If the investigator finds no discrimination, but thinks an alleged perpetrator's behavior created the appearance of discrimination, the investigator should provide appropriate coaching to the alleged perpetrator and advise his or her boss of the coaching.

If the investigator finds that discrimination did occur, the investigator should recommend appropriate remedial action to make the victim whole, and appropriate discipline for the perpetrator. In some companies, the investigator is empowered to remedy violations and to discipline wrongdoers; in other companies, the investigator makes recommendations to the bosses of the victim and the perpetrator, and those bosses make the final decisions. It is essential to have checks and balances to prevent condonation of discrimination. If the investigator does not have the authority to remedy the effects of bias (for example, to promote a woman who was passed over for promotion in favor of a man due to her gender), or to discipline a perpetrator of discrimination (for example, to discharge a manager who solicited sexual favors from a subordinate), then there must be a systematic method of escalating any difference of opinion between the investigator and the ultimate decision maker.

Rejection of the investigator's recommendation should require the approval of an officer of the company who was in no way implicated in the complaint. The reasons for deviating from the investigator's recommendations should be documented in the case file. Such deviations should be exceedingly rare, or the complaint process will quickly lose its credibility.

Sometimes the victim will ask that no action be taken against the perpetrator—perhaps because the victim is afraid of retaliation, or does not want to "make waves." However, the employer has no choice under the law. Discrimination, once established, must be corrected. Even if today's victim would not pursue a claim against the company, tomorrow's victim will—and the company's failure to take appropriate action after the first complaint will multiply the liability.

Once a final decision has been made regarding remedies for victims and discipline for perpetrators of discrimination, someone should be assigned the accountability for ensuring that the agreed corrective actions actually are implemented. Particularly in the case of discipline that has a future effective date (such as withholding next year's raise and bonus), the investigator or someone else outside the chain of command must follow up to make sure it happens.

ESSENTIAL ELEMENTS IN THE

DOCUMENTATION OF AN INVESTIGATION

- how and from whom the complaint was received

- what the complaint alleged

- which of the allegations, if established, would constitute a violation of equal employment opportunity laws or company policy

- whom the investigator interviewed

- what data or other documentary evidence the investigator analyzed

- a summary of the interview(s) of each witness

- the investigator's resolution of credibility disputes and reasons for crediting one version of the facts over another

- the investigator's findings and recommendations

- any difference of opinion between the investigator and the ultimate decision makers regarding relief for victims or punishment of perpetrators

- any follow up actions required, and confirmation that such actions were taken

---

Sometimes one investigation sparks another. For example, while investigating Sally's claim that Tom sexually harassed her, the investigator may hear that Tom also harassed Mary, or that Tom's boss knew of and condoned Tom's harassment of Sally and Mary, or that Tom had retaliated against Jane for having reported him to the company's discrimination hotline. Witnesses in an investigation may tell the investigator that other witnesses are gossiping about the case (in violation of the confidentiality rule). The investigator should treat each of these issues as though a new complaint had been filed; resolving an isolated complaint while ignoring patterns of alleged misconduct would leave the company vulnerable to class action litigation.

A thorny issue is *how much to tell employees* other than the complainant, victim and alleged perpetrator. Should other witnesses be told the outcome of the investigation? Should coworkers of the complainant or victim be informed? There are competing concerns here. The more you tell employees, the more you expose the company to defamation claims from the alleged perpetrator and breach of privacy claims from witnesses and victims. But if you say little or nothing, employees may believe the company's discrimination complaint process is ineffective, and employees with legitimate complaints may go directly to court.

In a case where discrimination is found, the best compromise may be to tell everyone who was *interviewed* (including the complainant and any alleged victim) that the allegations of discrimination were corroborated, that the victim will be made whole, and that the wrongdoer will be disciplined. The victim, of course, will be advised of the details of his or her remedy (such as back pay, a transfer or promotion), but even the victim shouldn't be given any details about the discipline imposed on the perpetrator.

If the company has an employee newsletter, it's a good idea to report periodically on the types of complaints received by the internal investigators, the overall findings in those cases, and the actions taken to remedy any discrimination. These articles should not disclose the identities of the parties involved, nor details about the cases that would enable employees to determine who made the complaint or who was found to have engaged in discriminatory conduct.

The company should periodically audit the results of internal complaint investigations to see if there are any trends within or across organizations that may require systemic correction, rather than case-by-case fixes.

Knowing that there is an effective complaint mechanism should encourage employees to give the company the opportunity to resolve alleged discrimination internally rather than going "outside" to the media, customers, legislators, shareholders, unions or the courts.

Chapter 7—How To Deal Effectively With The Media In The Context Of Allegations Of Discrimination

As illustrated by the Tough Togs hypothetical in Chapter 1, it's important to have a plan for responding to media inquiries on discrimination complaints. Without a plan in place, the tendency is to react instinctively, and this is an area where instincts should be stifled.

The company's lawyers may advise you to give a "no comment" response to any media inquiries about alleged discrimination, because any statements you do make may be used against you if the eventual testimony in court varies from your press comment in the slightest way. Plaintiffs' lawyers will collect press statements and use them in depositions and at trial to contradict the sworn statements of company witnesses. Accordingly, many companies do have a policy of refusing any comment on pending litigation. While this may maximize their chances of succeeding in litigation, a strict "no comment" approach may not satisfy the company's business needs.

If your company decides to give statements to the media, there are some traps to avoid. First, do not deny an allegation unless you have thoroughly investigated it. For example, if an employee alleges that the president of the company solicited sexual favors from her, don't automatically deny it happened. It may be true; or the president may have said something that was misconstrued. Either way, a flat denial will only encourage the media to do more sleuthing. Remember Presidential candidate Gary Hart's challenge to the media?

MEDIA TRAPS TO AVOID

- Don't make a blanket denial before your investigation is complete.

- Don't give details.

- Don't contradict the challenger's details.

- Develop and stick to your positive message points:

  o your commitment to equal employment opportunity

  o your commitment to investigate and correct any violations of law or company policy

  o your favorable equal employment opportunity and affirmative action record

---

In fact, it's a bad idea ever to give details to the press, or to challenge details of alleged discrimination, because journalists thrive on controversy. They will try to prove you wrong (or find people who will give interviews contradicting you), and there will be more stories as a result. Every time your company's name is mentioned in a story about alleged discrimination, your public image will suffer—regardless of the actual content of the story. Your objective is to minimize the frequency of media coverage of any discrimination complaints. The less you say, the better.

As for *what* to say, it's important not to inadvertently buy into the complainant's theme. For example, if a female employee claims that a male coworker got the promotion she sought due to gender discrimination, the employer's natural tendency would be to tell the media the ways in which the woman's qualifications were inferior to the man's. The problem with this approach is that the public is likely to disbelieve the company's factual assertions and conclude that the woman was, in fact, discriminated against. This may not be fair, but it is reality. The public sees the employee as David and the company as Goliath. By directly contradicting an employee's factual allegations, the employer inadvertently reinforces those very claims.

So what *should* you tell the media, if "no comment" is insufficient? Tell them you are committed to equal employment opportunity and that your company takes full responsibility for preventing discrimination to the extent possible and correcting it when it does occur. Promise to conduct a full investigation of the allegations and to remedy any violation of law, which may be discovered.

Then make a quick segue to your company's "good news" stories about equal employment opportunity and affirmative action successes. For example, if the claim is one of race discrimination, and minorities are well represented at high levels in your company, tell the press about that. If the claim is sexual harassment, tell the press about your company's zero-tolerance policy. In other words, pick a theme that you would be happy to have the media report and turn every interview into an opportunity to tell your story. Put out press releases or press responses along the same lines. This may annoy reporters, but making friends with the press is not your objective.

Don't forget that your employees watch the news and read magazines, and they are your ambassadors. Employees should never learn about your company in the public media. Once you know a story will be published or aired, you should inform your employees—especially if the story is expected to be negative. Treat your employees as part of your team, so they will trust you and be less likely to take your adversary's side in a publicized discrimination dispute. Keeping your employees informed might be as easy as faxing a copy of the company's press releases to all work locations at the same time they go out to the media. Or you may need to have the CEO send a letter to every employee explaining the company's position.

At the same time, it's crucial not to try to stage employee support for the company's position, for example, by planting letters to the editor or callers to a radio talk show, or by organizing a protest of the Equal Employment Opportunity Commission's offices. Such tactics are generally perceived as coercive, intimidating, and "further proof" of the company's guilt.

It's a mistake to wait until the media come to you with allegations of discrimination to tell them your "good news" stories. Every time a woman or minority is hired or promoted into a high level position, put out a press release. Look for opportunities to have women and minority employees (especially high-level managers) participate in news programs, industry conferences that will be covered by the media, and other highly visible events. Don't ignore minority media outlets. For example, if you have an African American executive, ask the local African American-owned radio station to invite him or her to a talk show to discuss any issue relevant to your company. And remember to place some of your ads with minority-owned media.

If your company has established minority scholarships, been listed among the best companies for women to work for, won an award for minority business subcontracting, or otherwise contributed to minority causes, don't hesitate to advertise your good deeds—on your World Wide Web page, in press releases, and in proactive contacts with the media (including the minority media). Consider "branding" your philanthropy a la "AT&T We Care" or "Ronald McDonald House."

By taking these proactive steps, when a "bad news" story rears its ugly head, the media will already have a file on your company filled with factual information that rebuts the inference that you are guilty of discrimination. While this may not "kill" a story, it may make the reporter (or the reporter's editor) less likely to trash your company— or more likely to publish your "good news" response.

In the event your internal investigation of a bias complaint concludes that discrimination occurred, and you are contacted by the media for a comment on the results of your investigation, consult with your legal counsel to see if there is a way publicly to acknowledge the error that was made and the general nature of the corrective action to be taken, without exposing the company to liability to the victim. Conversely, if your investigation concludes that no discrimination occurred, use the opportunity of any subsequent media inquiries to reinforce your commitment to equal employment opportunity.

Finally, you must accept the fact that no matter how successful you are at maintaining a discrimination-free workplace, disgruntled employees, vendors, customers, or unions will play the discrimination card to achieve their selfish goals; and sometimes the media will publish their allegations. Some people will conclude that your company discriminates. However, unless a major lawsuit or allegations of high-level misconduct follow, your company probably will survive the bad publicity with little or no impact on your long-term reputation, sales or profitability.

CHAPTER 8—HOW TO REMEDY ACTUAL AND PERCEIVED DISCRIMINATION WHILE BUILDING TRUST WITH CUSTOMERS, INVESTORS, EMPLOYEES AND OTHER STAKEHOLERS

The preceding chapters have demonstrated how to minimize the likelihood of being sued for discrimination, and how to survive those claims that can't be avoided. Those are important goals because they protect not only your company's bank account, but also its intangible assets—your external reputation and your brand. Equally important, by creating and maintaining a fair workplace, your company can strengthen its bonds with its employees generally, reducing turnover and providing a competitive edge in recruitment.

Discriminatory conduct, when it happens and is discovered, must be dealt with swiftly and strictly. There is a tendency to be lenient to an otherwise good employee who has crossed the line—perhaps inadvertently. The employee's boss often will argue that a "single mistake" shouldn't end a person's career, particularly if the employee is contrite.

If the company's sole objective, or top priority, were to do what's "fair" to the perpetrators of discrimination, a mild penalty might be imposed. Resist that impulse! Preserving the career of an employee who broke the rules simply cannot be the goal. To be harsh, what is one "otherwise good" employee worth? What's the cost of replacing such an employee? Even with recruitment and training, any employee, at any level, can be replaced at a cost of two to 12 months' pay. If you have any employees who are "irreplaceable," all that means is that you have not done a good job of succession planning.

In comparison, losing a single-employee discrimination lawsuit typically costs a large company half a million dollars, including attorneys' fees for the plaintiff and the company. Class actions can go over $100 million.

Similarly, the risk of trying to rehabilitate an employee who has violated another employee's civil rights simply is too high. For any serious equal employment opportunity violation, discharge is the only appropriate penalty. For a less-serious violation, you must at the very least impose a significant financial penalty (such as a pay freeze and forfeiture of bonus). If the penalty you choose is something other than discharge, be sure to give the employee a final warning that any future violation of your non-discrimination policy will result in discharge.

The strongest argument in favor of discharge is that other penalties simply are invisible to the outside world, including other employees, advocacy groups, customers, and the general public. As far as these stakeholders are concerned, if you keep the employee on your payroll after he or she has violated another employee's civil rights, you are condoning the violation. It means you aren't serious about your non-discrimination policy. Some of your other, excellent, employees may leave because they don't want to work for an employer that does not take equal employment opportunity seriously. You can't be the employer of choice in the 21st Century if you are soft on discrimination.

In addition to punishing the wrongdoer, when you discover discrimination you must make the victim "whole." That means putting the victim in the same place he or she would have been but for the discrimination. If the victim has unfairly lost a promotion, that means promoting him or her, even if there is no longer an opening, and making up the difference in back pay. If the victim has had no tangible employment loss but has suffered credible embarrassment or emotional distress, you should offer some compensation. This may, but need not, be financial compensation. Sometimes an additional week or two of paid vacation to recover from the incident, or a lateral change in assignment or supervision, may be what the victim wants. Sometimes the victim wants the perpetrator to apologize—perhaps in front of the entire workgroup. It is appropriate to ask the victim (through his or her attorney, if represented) what it would take to restore the status quo that existed prior to the discriminatory acts. You may be surprised that the victim is not looking to get rich, just to have his or her claim validated and corrected.

Satisfying the victim is relatively painless when the victim is a model employee. Unfortunately, sometimes the victim is a mediocre employee, a union activist, or a general pain in the butt. Notwithstanding, you must make the victim whole. Otherwise, the victim may become a martyr, or a media darling.

Resist the temptation to fight a lawsuit when you have procedural or technical defenses—such as a statute of limitations—but the under-lying conduct violated the plaintiff's civil rights. Your lawyers will not like this paragraph because it is their job to find and pursue every eth-ical defense to liability. However, your reputation with your employ-ees generally and with your external stakeholders is more important than winning every case.

On the other hand, you must not give in to extortion. Just because an employee claims that he or she was the victim of discrimination does not mean it is so. As important as it is not to under-react to dis-crimination claims, you must not over-react. You must not confuse equal employment opportunity with political correctness.

For example, no law prohibits one employee from asking another employee out on a date:

> Sam: Hi, Sally. I was wondering if you'd like to go out for drinks after work one day this week.
>
> Sally: Oh, I'm busy this week.
>
> Sam: Well, how about next week? You name the day. I'd like to get to know you better.
>
> Sally: I don't think so. I'm just not interested in seeing you outside of work, Sam.
>
> Sam: Say no more. I won't bring it up again.

Assuming Sam keeps his word and never raises the subject again, and he takes no actions against Sally for refusing his overture, no law has been broken. Your company policy shouldn't prohibit this kind of exchange. To try to prohibit such lawful conduct because of fear of harassment complaints is substituting political correctness for good judgment, and will alienate your employees.

Similarly, avoid jumping to the conclusion that all allegations of discrimination are true, or that discrimination claims should be settled without regard to their merits. Such over-reaction has the predictable effect of encouraging future extortion attempts by the same employees, their attorneys and coworkers.

The bottom line is that there is no substitute for the exercise of good judgment. Each claim must be evaluated on its merits and appropriate action must be taken. The best rule of thumb is to ask how you would feel if your response to the discrimination claim were published on the front page of your local newspaper. If you would be satisfied that the public would find your actions within the zone of reasonableness, you have made the right decision.

Most important, you want your employees to know that you can be trusted—that you clearly articulate the rules of conduct and then enforce those rules consistently. If you meet that standard in your employees' eyes, they will be your ambassadors to the world at large. Your employees will read about some other company's major discrimination case and say (to themselves and each other), "that would never happen here."

IV. SPECIAL CHALLENGES OF THE 21ST CENTURY

CHAPTER 9—THE INTERNET AND E-MAIL AS VEHICLES FOR HARASSMENT

In almost all workplaces in the United States, employees use computers and have access to electronic mail (e-mail), and often to the Internet as well.

A recurring problem that developed near the end of the 1990s and which continues today is the use of e-mail and the Internet at work to access pornography and to circulate jokes and cartoons—some of which are pornographic and some of which are racist, sexist, or otherwise violate non-discrimination standards.

Sometimes an offensive e-mail is forwarded inadvertently to an unintended recipient, who is offended and files a complaint.

What distinguishes these cases from those involving non-electronic communications is the ease and speed with which electronic messages are shared. By the time the company receives and investigates a claim that Pat forwarded a racist joke to Don, a dozen other employees may have received the same e-mail from Pat. Some of those recipients may have forwarded the e-mail to other coworkers, and so forth. The problem usually is huge by the time it is noticed.

It is only a matter of time before class action lawsuits are filed complaining of Internet/e-mail based harassment. Perhaps a case of this type will be in the news by the time this book is published.

What's the solution? To block e-mails? That's not practical. It may even be impractical to block access to pornographic web sites, because software that controls Internet access often blocks useful sites as well. In any event, computer-savvy employees can disable the blocking software, or use the computer's modem to access e-mail and the

Internet without going through your company's access-protected servers.

Rather, you should develop and implement an appropriate policy on the use of the Internet and e-mail at work. A key element of such a policy is to inform employees that they have no right of privacy when they use the company's e-mail or Internet access. Here is a sample policy:

PERSONAL USE OF COMPANY COMPUTER EQUIPMENT AND INTERNET ACCESS

Introduction: The Company's computer equipment and Internet access connections are for business use. Occasional incidental personal use is permitted, as described below. This policy is subject to change at any time.

No Privacy Rights: When you use the Company's computer equipment and/or Internet access, you waive any claim of privacy. The Company may monitor your use, including keeping a record of all Internet sites you visit. The Company may read, copy, and disclose to others the content of any files on your Company-provided computer including e-mails you send and receive. By using the Company's computer equipment and/or Internet connections, you consent to such monitoring, reading, copying and disclosure.

Downloading Prohibited: You must not download onto the Company's computer equipment any games, plug-ins, software, or other executable files from the Internet or from CDs, floppy diskettes or other media.

Unsuitable Subject Matter: You must not access any Internet site which contains unsuitable subject matter, including, but not limited to:

- sexually explicit ("adult") content, including but not limited to pornography or "personal" advertisements for sexual encounters
- gambling, including lotteries, raffles, and betting on sports events
- violence, illegal drugs or other illegal goods or activities
- jokes, cartoons or other content inconsistent with the Company's non-discrimination policy

In addition to avoiding Internet sites with such content, you must not use the Company's computer equipment, or the Company's Internet access, to send any e-mails with such content. If you receive any e-mail on the Company's computer equipment or through the Company's Internet access which includes such unsuitable subject matter, you must immediately delete it, and not save, copy, print, or forward it to anyone (including forwarding it to yourself at any personal e-mail account you may have). You are also prohibited from sending or forwarding chain letters, humor, prayers, charitable or business solicitations, and political petitions, regardless of whether these messages contain unsuitable subject matter.

Frequency and Duration of Personal Use: Your personal use of the Company's computer equipment and/or Internet access must be limited so as not to interfere with your performance of your job. For example, taking one minute to send an e-mail to a child at college generally would be permissible, while spending fifteen minutes shopping for a gift on-line during working hours generally would be impermissible. If in doubt as to whether your frequency or duration of personal use exceeds what is permissible, it is your obligation to ask your supervisor.

Disclaimer: If you send any non-business message on a Company computer and/or Internet access addressed to a public group, government official or other company or organization, you must indicate in the message that that the views expressed are yours and do not reflect the Company's official position.

Violations: Violations of this policy subject you to discipline, up to and including dismissal.

You may want to break your policy up into smaller pieces and publish it as a booklet or pamphlet. Employees should be required to sign an acknowledgment that they have read the policy and they understand it.

After developing and implementing such a policy, you must enforce it vigorously—even if it means firing dozens or hundreds of employees if that many are involved in forwarding objectionable material on your e-mail system. The good news is that after one such calamity, the remaining employees are unlikely to violate the e-mail/Internet policy.

If you are aware of widespread use of your computer facilities to transmit racially or sexually offensive material, and you don't take strong action, you may as well get out your checkbook and start writing that multi-million dollar check to the class-action plaintiffs' law firm. And while you're at it, start looking for replacements for your fair-minded employees who won't want to work for you anymore.

CHAPTER 10—"TEMPS" AND OTHER CONTINGENT WORKERS AS PERPETRATORS OR VICTIMS OF DISCRIMINATION

These days, most companies supplement their workforces with employees from an agency ("temps"), who typically work assignments shorter than a year, as well as with independent contractors and other "contingent" workers who may stay a year or longer but are not on the company's payroll. Among the many legal issues raised by these arrangements is the extent of the company's responsibility for discrimination perpetrated by, or suffered by, these workers. Consider the following example:

Bob, a night guard who works for a security company, sexually harasses Jill, a regular full-time employee of your company. Is your company liable? Perhaps. Did you have any control over Bob's work? Did one of your company managers supervise Bob's performance? Did your company have the right to control how Bob did his work? Did your company have the right to hire, fire, and discipline Bob? If so, your company probably is at least a "joint employer" of Bob, and possibly Bob's actual "common law" employer. The fact that Bob is on the payroll of the security company is not determinative. It's likely that you will be held as responsible—and liable—for Bob's conduct as if he were your direct employee.

Even if a manager who works for the security company supervises Bob, and you are not found to be Bob's employer, you still can be found responsible for his harassment of your employee, Jill. That's because it's your obligation to provide Jill with a harassment-free

91

workplace. If you had any prior knowledge that Bob had engaged in discriminatory conduct, and you failed to take appropriate remedial action, you are at fault.

What should you do if an employee complains that a "temp" or some other "contingent" worker discriminated against him or her? You could conduct a complete investigation, including interviewing the alleged perpetrator (if he or she will talk to you). On the other hand, you do not owe the "temp" or "contingent" worker any due process. Unless there is a provision to the contrary in your contract with the security company, you can simply tell them to replace Bob with someone else.

Should you tell Bob's agency why you want him replaced? Absolutely not! If you do, your company is likely to be sued for defamation. Your lawyers will tell you that you should be able to defend Bob's suit successfully—either because you can prove that he discriminated against Jill, or at least you can show that you had a legitimate business purpose for talking to Bob's agency about the allegations. In defamation law, this is called a "conditional privilege," and as long as you didn't have actual malice and didn't tell more people than necessary, you should win. However, there's a chance the court will find that someone in your company acted with malice (which can be nothing more than knowledge of the falsity of the allegations of discrimination, or reckless indifference as to whether the allegations were false). Or the court may find that the allegations about Bob were shared with more people in your company or more people at the security company than necessary. And you may then be stuck with an adverse judgment for hundreds of thousands of dollars. Even if you win the defamation case, you will have substantial attorneys' fees.

So keep it simple. Just tell Bob's agency that you no longer want Bob, and politely decline to give a reason.

In the preceding examples, the victim was your employee, and the perpetrator was a "temp" or other "contingent" worker. What if it's the other way around, as in the following example?

Victor is referred to your company by an agency to work as a "temp" in your communications department—a group that reports to Mary, who is a regular full-time manager on your payroll. A few hours into Victor's first workday, Mary calls the agency and tells them to replace Victor with someone else. Mary declines to give a reason.

The next day, the agency sends Tom instead of Victor. Mary calls the agency again and tells them to send someone else. Mary accepts the third "temp," Francine.

Victor files a complaint with your internal investigator, claiming gender discrimination. He points out that he, and Tom, were better qualified than Francine, and that Mary has no men working for her in the entire communications department. Should your internal investigator conduct an investigation?

Absolutely! The issue here is whether your employee, Mary, has violated the law or your company policy against discrimination. You should investigate such a case just as if the victim were on your payroll. If the allegations are corroborated, you should take the same disciplinary action against Mary as you would have taken if she had discriminated against a fellow employee.

What about Victor? What about Tom? Do you make them whole? Yes. Talk to their agency and find out if they lost any days of work between assignments after Mary instructed the agency to replace them. If so, offer, through their agency, to make them whole. The situation is more complicated if the "temps" claim intangible losses, such as mental distress. But the principle is the same: make them whole.

Your lawyers may balk. After all, you have substantial defenses to a claim that Victor might bring before a government agency or in court. You could establish that you were not Victor's employer, or "joint" employer. Victor might claim that even if he was not your employee, your company is liable for interfering with his relationship with his agency. However that technical dispute might be resolved, you run the risk of adverse publicity if in fact Mary was discriminating against men. You also need to consider your own direct employees. If they are aware of Victor's complaint, they are watching closely to see if you make things right. For all of these reasons, you should satisfy Victor's reasonable demands for compensation and maintain the integrity of your non-discrimination policy.

The best damage control in cases brought by "temps" and other "contingent" workers is the same as in cases brought by regular employees. If you were wrong, compensate the victims fairly and correct the conditions that allowed the discriminatory conduct to occur.

In the examples above, the victims brought individual claims. However, with the proliferation of "contingent" worker arrangements, class action discrimination suits from non-payroll workers now are a serious risk. Even facially neutral policies and procedures that have a perceived detrimental impact on "contingent" workers compared to your regular employees may be challenged as discriminatory. For example, if your production employees (mostly men) are on your payroll and receive health care and pension benefits, while your office workers (mostly women) are "contingent" workers on the payroll of an agency and receive no health care or pension benefits, you may get a class action lawsuit from the office workers claiming gender discrimination.

Add one more background fact: Years ago, when fringe benefits were cheap, the office workers were on your payroll. When health care costs began to rise dramatically in the 1980s, you "contracted out" the office work to the agency to save money, knowing that the agency did not provide benefits to its employees but was still able to recruit qualified clericals because most of them had husbands who got family health benefits at their jobs elsewhere. Yes, you may be able to defend such a case successfully based upon the lack of an actual employment relationship between you and the office workers. But even if the class action lawsuit is thrown out of court, you may lose in the eyes of your employees, your customers and your community.

When you defend actions, which seem discriminatory to neutral observers, you draw your company's ethical values into question. If your response to an allegation of discrimination starts with the phrase, "yes, but" the price of winning simply is too high.

Chapter 11—Religion In The Workplace; One Employee's Religious Expression Is Another's Harassment

Gary, your company's internal investigator of bias claims, has seen an up tick in the frequency of complaints of religious harassment. In years past, Gary would occasionally receive a complaint from an employee who had been denied time off for religious observance, and Gary was usually able to find a satisfactory solution by coaching the employee's bosses to ask for someone to swap shifts. But recent claims have focused on an altogether different issue—the extent to which employees can practice their religion in the workplace.

Just last week, Gary got three new complaints:

Tony, a lay preacher, composes a one-minute inspirational Christian message every morning, which he sends through the company's voice mail system to coworkers who have asked to be on his distribution. Last week, Tony added a number to his distribution list, which is a digit off from the phone number of the colleague who wanted to receive the message. The actual recipient does not share Tony's religious views and filed a complaint asserting that it's inappropriate for Tony to use company facilities for religious expression. Gary agreed with the complainant and instructed Tony to stop sending the daily messages over the company's voice mail system.

Tony objected, claiming that Matt, the company's Director of Diversity, had specifically asked to be on Tony's voice-mail distribution list, and had complimented Tony on some of the messages. In fact, Matt had forwarded some of the messages to members of the Senior

Management team. Gary called Matt to confirm this and got Matt's voice mail greeting, which ends with, "Have a blessed day!"

Meanwhile, Kim, who is an advocate for gay rights, filed a complaint about a group of employees who formed a gospel choir. They practice in an empty conference room at lunchtime and occasionally perform at retirement parties if the retiring employee so requests. Kim asserted that because these fundamentalist Christians believe that homosexuals are sinners, allowing them to rehearse and perform at work is an endorsement of hatred of homosexuals and therefore violates Kim's religious beliefs. Gary investigated and found that the choir welcomed singers of any religion, that the choir specifically avoided hymns that mentioned Christ, and that none of the choir members considered homosexuals to be sinners.

Also last week, Gary got a fax from JoAnn, complaining about her boss, Harold, who begins staff meetings with a moment of silence, which he concludes by saying "Amen." Gary coached Harold not to have the moment of silence, but Harold pointed out that Regina, the CFO, always says Grace aloud in the cafeteria before eating lunch, and some employees at her table and tables nearby join in the prayer or a final "Amen."

The common theme in all of these examples is that religious expression in the workplace pits employees against each other. It may be necessary to inhibit the religious expression of some employees in order to satisfy the interest of their coworkers in being free of unwanted religious influence or perceived pressure.

The law in this area is evolving. Clearly, employees cannot be forced to practice a religion, say a prayer, or advocate any particular religious beliefs, in order to get or keep a job, a promotion, or a raise. Just as clearly, a boss or coworker can't show disrespect for another employee's religion or religious beliefs. What is unclear is whether allowing employees to express their own religious views—which is an obligation of some religions—should or must be curtailed in order to protect their coworkers' desire to be free from being proselytized.

Until the courts clarify rights and obligations in this area, it is prudent to impose sufficient restrictions on religious expression to avoid *class-action* claims. That means precluding high-level managers from making *any* religious expression at work. The reason for imposing a religious gag order on high-level managers is that, given their positions of power, the inference of coercion will be difficult, if not impossible, to rebut in litigation. And if a claim is filed, the potential class size is large because executives have high visibility.

Similarly, the company should prohibit the use of company facilities—such as e-mail, voice mail, or performances on company premises—to "broadcast" messages with religious content. All of these can raise class-based claims of religious harassment due to the inference that higher management endorses these messages.

At the other end of the spectrum, it probably is *not* necessary to place a "gag" order on non-supervisory employees, for example prohibiting the saying of Grace at meals. Although coworkers may complain, there is no inherent coercion from peers, and in any event there is no likely affected class of victims to bring a class action.

CONCLUSION

THE NEUTRON BOMB CAN BE DEFUSED

If you are fortunate enough to be reading this book before your company has been sued in a class action discrimination suit, you can take steps to reduce your risk. You can immunize your company from the class-action flu by adopting and enforcing strong policies prohibiting unlawful discrimination. This is more than a paper exercise. You must train your employees on equal employment opportunity and evaluate them on their compliance with the policy. You need to conduct periodic audits. You must have an effective internal complaint investigation process, which not only resolves the individual claims as they arise, but also identifies and corrects root causes.

Above all, ensure that everyone who works for or with your company is treated with respect and as a member of the team. There is no stronger motivator for class action discrimination suits than a perception of disrespect—of "us versus them." The entire "diversity" movement is grounded in the concept of respecting and including all employees in making the business a success, recognizing that each employee is an individual whose differences from other employees can add value.

When you manage your employees—your human resources—with integrity, you encourage them to conduct your business with integrity. When you take the moral high road, you attract people of strong moral fiber. When you show your loyalty to your employees by protecting them from unfair treatment at the hands of their bosses, they repay you with loyalty (so you don't lose them to competitors, even when you have a bad year and can't offer raises).

If your employees don't already have a union, the single most important thing you can do to keep it that way is to show your employees, every day, that they do not need a union to be treated fairly.

If the vast majority of your employees trust and respect your company as a fair place to work, no malcontented coworker, and no lawyer, will be able to motivate them to bring a class action against you.

Notwithstanding all of these efforts, you may still get a class action. The case may be motivated by ulterior interests—perhaps a competitor, a union seeking to organize your employees, or a public interest group looking for a high-visibility target. Regardless, you must be prepared to respond, not only in the courtroom, but also in the media, with your own employees, and with any other important stakeholders. You should have a plan of action developed now, just as you do for other contingencies like product recalls or terrorism. The plan should include immediately convening an interdisciplinary crisis management team comprised of senior executives and outside expert consultants. The first hours of a crisis are when most mistakes are compounded, so delay is usually very costly.

If you've taken all the appropriate steps to prevent class actions, then you should be able to defend one successfully—while maintaining your reputation and the value of your brand. You can defuse that neutron bomb.

ABOUT THE AUTHOR

Charles M. Carron grew up in Tampa where he attended the Berkeley Preparatory School before earning his undergraduate degree from Princeton and his law degree from Stanford. Mr. Carron subsequently trained as a mediator, specializing in workplace dispute resolution.

After three years with the law firm Squire, Sanders & Dempsey, Mr. Carron became an in-house labor attorney for the Bell System and worked his way up to senior manager of Bell Atlantic and then Verizon Communications—companies recognized for their successful affirmative action programs.

Mr. Carron now has his own practice limited to employment law, mediation and management consulting (www.carronlaw.com). He also consults with the crisis management firm of Rowan & Blewitt Incorporated (www.rowanblewitt.com).

Mr. Carron wrote this book out of a deep sense of frustration over the inept and sometimes tragic ways that some other notable companies have attracted, and then reacted to, discrimination suits. In this book, he explains how companies, just like individuals, can learn and practice respect for differences—and thereby defuse the discrimination bomb, while creating a workplace that is fair to all.

Mr. Carron resides in Arlington, Virginia, and can be reached at carron2@msn.com or (703) 838-0321.